TABLE OF CONTENTS

INTRODUCTION

Two years on from the bloody and destructive suicide attack on a United Nations (U.N.) facility in Abuja, Nigeria, the Nigerian terrorist organization Boko Haram continues to pose a threat to both the United States and our allies. Since that attack, Boko Haram has received increased international attention, has carried out near-daily attacks throughout much of Nigeria, and has taken part in operations in other parts of West Africa. They remain a lethal and growing threat to the people of Nigeria, the international community, Americans in the region, and potentially the United States Homeland.

As on August 26, 2011, there is much we still do not know about Boko Haram or their splinter group Ansaru, which emerged in 2012. The exact details of their operations, size, and structure remain a mystery, and a solution to the defeating them remains elusive. Yet, despite these persistent gaps, this Committee has come to learn a great deal about Boko Haram, their goals, resources, and allies, and has identified steps the United States can take to address this threat.

On November 30, 2011, the Committee on Homeland Security Subcommittee on Counterterrorism and Intelligence released a report entitled, "Boko Haram – Emerging Threat to the U.S. Homeland," which detailed the history of, and danger posed by, Boko Haram. On the same day, the Subcommittee also held a hearing to examine the threat of Boko Haram and of terrorists across the Sahel region of West Africa. Members of this Committee, including then-Subcommittee Chairman Patrick Meehan and Full Committee Chairman Peter King, have written several times to the Department of State urging the Secretary to designate Boko Haram a Foreign Terrorist Organization (FTO). On May 17, 2012, Congressman Meehan also introduced the "Boko Haram Terrorist Designation Act of 2012," a version of which became law as an amendment to the National Defense Authorization Act for Fiscal Year 2013.

Each of these efforts has been designed to raise awareness of the threat Boko Haram poses to the United States, and provide solutions to the increasingly grave challenges we face in Nigeria and throughout western Africa.

This report – a follow up to "Boko Haram – Emerging Threat to the U.S. Homeland," – provides even greater detail on the evolution of Boko Haram into an increasingly sophisticated ally of al Qaeda; elaborates courses of action open to the United States and our partners; and makes the case for Boko Haram to be listed as an FTO. In a diversified threat environment where multiple al Qaeda affiliates and allies (as well as other terror networks) are taking advantage of security deficiencies throughout the Middle East and Africa, it is vital that we anticipate and address all emerging terror threats, before they reach the United States. This includes lethal networks that fall outside of our historical notion of al Qaeda affiliates.

Boko Haram is just one example of the multiple terror threats proliferating throughout Africa that increasingly challenge the security of U.S. interests and the U.S. Homeland. As the Committee hopes to demonstrate in this report, these and other dangers will require increased attention not only on all of Africa, but also demand coordinated, and agile interagency analysis and response. Boko Haram's surprisingly rapid progression into a sophisticated, lethal force should serve as a warning to those who would answer the nation's current fiscal constraints with a retreat from the continent, and a turn away from the advances we have made in our counterterrorism efforts over the last twelve years.

As an update to the Committee's 2011 study of Boko Haram, this report is based on open-source information and extensive unclassified research and briefings from government and non-government entities. Academic research and expert knowledge of Boko Haram has struggled to keep pace with the group's rapid evolution. This report attempts to further enhance the popular understanding of their lethality, operations, and relationship with al Qaeda. It is the Committee's hope that the recommendations outlined in this report will assist the United States and the broader international community in defeating Boko Haram and safeguarding American persons and interests in Nigeria and throughout the world.

MICHAEL T. McCAUL
Chairman
Committee on Homeland Security

PATRICK L. MEEHAN
Chairman
Subcommittee on Cybersecurity,
Infrastructure Protection, and
Security Technologies

PETER T. KING
Chairman
Subcommittee on
Counterterrorism and
Intelligence

FINDINGS

1. BOKO HARAM HAS EVOLVED INTO AN AL QAEDA ALLY THROUGH THEIR CONNECTIONS WITH AL QAEDA IN THE LANDS OF THE ISLAMIC MAGHREB (AQIM) AND AL SHABAAB.

2. BOKO HARAM'S ANTAGONIZATION OF NIGERIAN CHRISTIANS AND MUSLIM CRITICS THREATENS THE STABILITY OF NIGERIA BY RISKING RELIGIOUS CIVIL WAR. THIS WOULD FURTHER DESTABILIZE WEST AFRICA, A REGION ALREADY UNDERGOING SEVERE DISTRESS.

3. BOKO HARAM'S ACTIVITY BEYOND NIGERIA'S BORDERS NOW REQUIRES ENHANCING THE CAPABILITY OF NEIGHBORING STATES SUCH AS CHAD, CAMEROON, AND NIGER TO DEFEAT THE THREAT. THIS VIOLENCE IS NO LONGER AFFECTING NIGERIA ALONE, BUT HAS BECOME A REGIONAL THREAT.

4. THE DESIGNATION OF 3 BOKO HARAM MEMBERS AS SPECIALLY DESIGNATED GLOBAL TERRORISTS (SDGT) IS NOT ENOUGH TO PREVENT PERSONS WITHIN U.S. JURISDICTION FROM AIDING BOKO HARAM. A FOREIGN TERRORIST ORGANIZATION (FTO) DESIGNATION IS REQUIRED, AND MAKES A NECESSARY STATEMENT ABOUT HOW THE U.S. PERCEIVES BOKO HARAM. IT WILL ALSO LEND SUPPORT TO SIMILAR ACTIONS TAKEN BY THE UNITED KINGDOM AND THE GOVERNMENT OF NIGERIA.

RECOMMENDATIONS

1. **DESIGNATE BOKO HARAM A FOREIGN TERRORIST ORGANIZATION (FTO):** The Secretary Of State must recognize Boko Haram and their splinter group Ansaru as FTOs – as formally requested by the Department of Justice and this Committee. This would provide Federal agencies with the tools they need to assist our partners in defeating Boko Haram and would provide clear guidance on how the United States views the threat the group poses.

2. **DO NOT UNDERESTIMATE BOKO HARAM'S INTENT AND CAPABILITY TO ATTACK THE U.S. HOMELAND:** The U.S. Intelligence Community risks repeating the mistakes made with Tehrik-e-Taliban Pakistan (TTP) and al Qaeda in the Arabian Peninsula (AQAP) in failing to recognize the threat these groups posed until after each attempted to attack the U.S. Homeland. Boko Haram and its splinter group Ansaru have proven themselves as increasingly sophisticated and equally ruthless killers. Boko Haram, Ansaru, and al Qaeda are unified by an ideology that justifies horrific violence and views the United States as an enemy and a target.

3. **INCREASE U.S. INTELLIGENCE COMMUNITY COLLECTION ON BOKO HARAM AND OTHER TERRORIST ORGANIZATIONS IN SUB-SAHARAN AFRICA:** In recent years, al Qaeda affiliates and allies have dramatically increased their presence and operational activity throughout Africa. This has left the United States and our allies faced with an increasingly diverse and deadly adversary, in an environment with limited resources to combat the threat.

4. **INCREASE U.S. GOVERNMENT ASSISTANCE TO REGIONAL COUNTERTERRORISM AND INTELLIGENCE PROGRAMS:** Our partners throughout the region will require our assistance in meeting their security needs. The United States, working through our Department of State and Africa Command (AFRICOM) will be increasingly called upon to develop the counterterrorism, law enforcement, and intelligence capacity of regional allies like Nigeria.

I.

ORIGINS AND HISTORY

Uprising

"Boko Haram," is the popular name for the Nigerian terrorist organization "Jama'atul Alhul Sunnah Lidda'wati wal Jihad," or "people committed to the propagation of the Prophet's teachings and jihad."[1] Though not an official moniker, the term Boko Haram is a revealing window into the ideology that drives the organization. It can be translated as "Western Education is forbidden," but according to many experts, the term goes beyond simply secular schooling and means a rejection of Western civilization and institutions.

Likely founded in the mid-1990's as a religious study group, Boko Haram did not begin to transform into the insurgent group it is today until a young and charismatic Nigerian Islamic cleric named Mohammed Yusuf assumed control. Calling themselves the Nigerian Taliban, Boko Haram adopted a "live-off-the land" lifestyle and established a camp in a remote area of northeast Nigeria, which the group dubbed "Afghanistan."[2]

From the early 2000's to 2009, Boko Haram engaged in low-level conflict with local police forces and non-compliant villagers. In 2009, a crackdown on Boko Haram members from Nigerian police forces in Borno state erupted into fighting. On July 26, 2009, sect members launched an attack against a police station in Bauchi state, resulting in the death of 39 Boko Haram members, two police officers, and one soldier.[3] This ignited a five day stand-off between Boko Haram and security personnel that saw violent attacks and battles spread across the three northern Nigerian states of Bauchi, Kano, and Yobe, and culminated in a final battle in the city of Maiduguri in Borno state.

On July 30, 2009, the battle of Maiduguri ended when Nigerian security forces captured and killed Boko Haram's leader, Mohammed Yusuf, in what human rights groups have deemed an extrajudicial killing. Yusuf's execution was videotaped by soldiers and later broadcast on television.[4] In total, nearly 700 people were killed in the uprising. The death of Yusuf marked a turning point for Boko Haram and forced the group underground. Many of its leaders reportedly fled to other parts of Nigeria, including Bauchi state, as well as countries throughout Africa.[5]

Radical Reemergence

In 2010, Boko Haram re-emerged, radically more violent and determined to seek vengeance against the Nigerian state for the execution of Mohammed Yusuf. Under the leadership of Imam Abubakar Shekau, who assumed control of the sect following

---

[1] "Boko Haram," Toni Johnson, *Council on Foreign Relations*, November 7, 2011. Available at: http://www.cfr.org/africa/boko-haram/p25739.

[2] "Boko Haram: History, ideas, and revolt [5]." Shehu Sani, *Vanguard*, July 7, 2011. Available at: http://www.vanguardngr.com/2011/07/boko-haram-history-ideas-and-revolt-5/.

[3] "Boko Haram: History, ideas, and revolt [4]." Shehu Sani, *Vanguard*, July 8, 2011. Available at: http://www.vanguardngr.com/2011/07/boko-haram-history-ideas-and-revolt-4/.

[4] Johnson, *supra* note 1.

[5] "Nigeria Conflict Assessment," USAID, August 2011, pg. 39.

Yusuf's death, Boko Haram militants carried out violent operations against government targets in the North. The most notable include the September 2010 assault on a Maiduguri prison that resulted in the release of 700 prisoners, including Boko Haram members, and a bombing in the city of Jos that killed more than 80 people. Significantly, the targeting of the Nigerian capital city of Abuja represented an evolving threat outside of Boko Haram's native northeastern Nigeria. In June 2011, Boko Haram militants bombed the police headquarters in Abuja and two months later carried out a well-publicized suicide attack against the nearby United Nations headquarters. Despite the international outcry following the U.N. bombing, Boko Haram's attacks have continued.

A number of factors have been attributed to the fueling of Boko Haram's violence and fanaticism, including a feeling of alienation from the more-developed, predominantly Christian, southern region of Nigeria; pervasive poverty; rampant government corruption; incompetent and brutal security services; and the belief that relations with the West are a corrupting influence. These grievances have led to sympathy for Boko Haram among the local Muslim population despite the group's violent tactics.[6] Residents of northern Nigeria live in extreme poverty. In Maiduguri, many residents live on less than two dollars a day.[7] Shettima Khalifa Dikwa, chairman of the Voters Forum at the University of Maiduguri, blamed the government and heavy security practices for the growing public sympathy toward Boko Haram. He said, "If it escalates it is the fault of the government and JTF (Joint Task Force). You can't have JTF searching your house, invading your privacy, mistreating people without you having sympathy for Boko Haram."[8] These grievances and the failure of the government to effectively address them serve as key recruiting tools for Boko Haram. Nonetheless, the crutch of "grievances" – however valid – hides a more dangerous reality. The evolution of Boko Haram from a group of disaffected Muslim youths to a ruthless and operationally savvy international terrorist network has been fueled by radical Islamism and al Qaeda's guidance.

Boko Haram claimed that their mission to implement *sharia law* and establish an Islamic state throughout all of Nigeria is a solution to the problems facing Nigeria's Muslims.[9] Yet, *sharia* law is currently observed in 12 out of 36 Nigerian states as the result of a grassroots movement that coincided with Nigeria's transition to democracy in 1999.[10]

Going Global

Boko Haram publicly embraced international jihad with their August 26, 2011 attack on a United Nations facility in Abuja, Nigeria, which killed approximately 23 people.[11] Though many dismiss Boko Haram as driven by local issues, such an audacious

---

[6] "In Nigeria's northeast, some sympathy for Islamists," Joe Brock, *Reuters*, November 14, 2011. Available at: http://in.reuters.com/article/2011/11/14/idINIndia-60515120111114.

[7] Ibid.

[8] Ibid.

[9] Johnson, *supra* note 1.

[10] Ibid.

[11] "Islamist sect Boko Haram claims Nigerian U.N. bombing," Ibrahim Mshelizza, *Reuters*, August 29, 2011. Available at: http://www.reuters.com/article/2011/08/29/us-nigeria-bombing-claim-idUSTRE77S3ZO20110829.

attack on the international community betrays the claim that their movement is merely "local." Indeed, over the last two years, they have only further demonstrated a willingness to strike non-Nigerian targets or to act outside of Nigeria, and even threaten media outlets in the United States.[12] In an episode that echoed AQIM's capture of Western hostages for ransom, a Boko Haram cell now known as Ansaru has been identified as responsible for the kidnapping of an Italian and a Briton in May 2011 – months before the U.N. bombing.[13] They were held for nearly a year before being killed by their captors during a joint rescue attempt conducted by British and Nigerian forces in the Nigerian city of Sokoto.[14]

In February 2013, Boko Haram kidnapped a European family in Cameroon.[15] It is believed that a ransom of three million dollars was paid to free the seven-person family, which included children. There are significant indications that the move was a reaction to French involvement in Mali. As recently as June 2013, the State Department, noting the threat of kidnappings and armed attacks in Nigeria, warned U.S. citizens "extremists could expand their operations beyond northern Nigeria to the country's middle and southern states."[16] The travel warning also references specific written threats received by U.S. citizen missionaries in northern Nigeria. These incidents illustrate that Boko Haram's target list is not restricted to the local population and presents significant threats to Westerners.

According to the *Washington Post*, members of Boko Haram have used "Niger as a gateway to join up with the Islamists in northern Mali," and "trying to spread [Boko Haram's] hard-line ideology and violent aspirations in these border towns…"[17] In a step forward, officials in Niger have worked with the Nigerian government to establish joint border patrols and facilitate greater cooperation.[18] Boko Haram is also reportedly active in Cameroon, where the kidnapping of the French family took place, and on October 20, 2012, the mayor of a Cameroonian border town was assassinated by Boko Haram while visiting Nigeria. These developments clearly provide Boko Haram with an international footprint that goes beyond local politics.

Speaking at the George Washington University's Homeland Security Policy Institute in December 2012, General Carter Ham, former Commander of U.S. Africa

---

[12] "In Nigeria, Boko Haram threatens attacks on media," *Committee to Protect Journalists*, September 24, 2012. Available at: http://cpj.org/2012/09/boko-haram-threatens-attacks-on-nigerian-news-outl.php.

[13] "Nigeria rescue bid: Kidnapped Briton and Italian killed," *BBC News*, March 4, 2011. Available at: http://www.bbc.co.uk/news/uk-17305707.

[14] "British and Italian hostages murdered by captors in special forces rescue bid in Nigeria," Matthew Holehouse, *The Telegraph*, March 8, 2012. Available at: http://www.telegraph.co.uk/news/worldnews/africaandindianocean/nigeria/9131785/British-and-Italian-hostages-murdered-by-captors-in-special-forces-rescue-bid-in-Nigeria.html.

[15] "Nigeria's Boko Haram 'got $3m ransom' to Free Hostages." *BBC News*, 26 April, 2013. Available at: http://www.bbc.co.uk/news/world-africa-22320077

[16] "Travel Warning" (Nigeria), *Bureau of Consular Affairs*, U.S. Department of State, June 3, 2013. Available at: http://travel.state.gov/travel/cis_pa_tw/tw/tw_5985.html

[17] "Niger struggles against Islamist militants," Sudarsan Raghavan, *The Washington Post,* August 16, 2011. Available at: http://www.washingtonpost.com/world/niger-struggles-against-militant-islam/2012/08/16/9b712956-d7f4-11e1-98c0-31f6f55bdc4a_graphic.html.

[18] "Niger, Nigeria Step Up Cooperation Against Boko Haram," Jacob Zenn, *World Politics Review,* October 31, 2012. Available at: http://www.worldpoliticsreview.com/articles/12463/niger-nigeria-step-up-cooperation-against-boko-haram.

Command (AFRICOM) compared Boko Haram's current status to that of al Qaeda in the 1990s. Summarizing their threat outside of Nigeria, General Ham said that "Boko Haram's leadership aspires to broader activities across the region, certainly to Europe, and I think, again, as their name implies, anything that is western is a legitimate target in their eyes."[19]

Composition and Leadership

According to a report released by the U.S. Department of Defense (DOD) Special Operations Command (SOCOM) Joint Special Operations University, Boko Haram's members are believed to be mostly ethnic Kanuri.[20] The Kanuri tribe comprises only 4 percent of the Nigerian population overall, and is concentrated in the northeastern Nigerian states of Bauchi and Borno. Because of Nigeria's porous borders and frequent movement between intertwined tribal communities Nigeria and neighboring states, "...there is evidence to suggest that these tribal relationships facilitate weapons trafficking and other cross-border smuggling transactions."[21]

According to the U.S. Congressional Research Service (CRS), the core group of Boko Haram militants "may number in the hundreds," but the organization also draws wide, informal support from a larger following of several thousand Nigerians, chiefly from the northeastern Kanuri tribe.[22]

Boko Haram is reportedly led by a Shura Council of thirty members that oversees and directs other cells.[23] Members of the Shura Council reportedly do not meet face-to-face frequently, but instead speak mostly via mobile phones. This absence of personal contact allows for a degree of anonymity amongst members and can lead to miscommunication between cells. According to a June 2012 report issued by the United States Institute for Peace (USIP), "Each member of the council is responsible for a cell, and each cell is focused on a different task or geographical area. Most of the group's actions are agreed at the council level, but Abubakar Shekau also takes decisions without referring them to the council."[24]

Obviously, this structure leaves Boko Haram open to division and provides little assurance that someone claiming to speak for the group is speaking for all of its factions. This has frequently proven to be the case, most noticeably in negotiation proceedings.[25] Shekau works with a few select cell leaders, maintaining little contact with Boko Haram operatives on the ground. It is possible that given this chaotic structure, various operatives may have little understanding of, or even concern for, whom they are taking orders from, making their actions more difficult to predict and, thus, more dangerous.

---

[19] "Counterterrorism in Africa," General Carter Ham speaking at The Homeland Security Policy Institute, December 3, 2012. Available at: http://www.gwumc.edu/hspi/events/GENHamPRF416.cfm.
[20] "Confronting the Terrorism of Boko Haram in Nigeria," James J.F. Forest, Ph.D., *The Joint Special Operations University,* May 05, 2012, pg. 1. Available at: http://www.jamesforest.com/wp-content/uploads/2012/06/Boko_Haram_JSOU-Report-2012.pdf
[21] Ibid.
[22] "Nigeria: Elections and Issues for Congress," Lauren Ploch, *U.S. Congressional Research Service,* January 19, 2012, pg. 14-15.
[23] "What is Boko Haram?" Andrew Walker, *United States Institute of Peace*, June 2012, pg. 8.
[24] Ibid., 8.
[25] Ibid., 11.

The confusion over Boko Haram's leadership is a significant gap in the United States' understanding of the organization. As we come to know more about who leads the network, it will be easier to understand Boko Haram's goals and, hopefully, defeat them.

Abubakar Shekau

Abubakar Shekau was an early follower of Mohammed Yusuf, Boko Haram's former leader, along with Mamman Nur, another group leader. However, according to Nigerian media sources, he is seen as the "most radical" of the three men.[26] Though much about Boko Haram's leadership remains unknown, Shekau himself has become a public figure. He is estimated to be in his mid-to-late thirties, and has held a fearless approach to running the group since assuming leadership.

Shekau has mimed Osama bin Laden in his video appearances by openly threatening the United States and every segment of Nigerian society, saying in one video, "I enjoy killing anyone that God commands me to kill – the way I enjoy killing chickens and rams." That statement, which appeared in a clip following an attack that killed at least 180 people in Kano, reveals Shekau's ruthlessness when planning operations.[27] For him, nothing is off limits.

Along with two others (Abubakar Adam Kambar, and Khalid al Barnawi), Abubakar Shekau is a Specially Designated Global Terrorist (SDGT), according to the United States. This designation was announced on June 21, 2012, and subjects any property or assets Shekau holds in U.S. jurisdictions to seizure.[28] Additionally, more recently, the United States placed a seven million dollar bounty on his capture, the highest of all African terror leaders.[29] In comparison, a bounty of only five million dollars was posted on Mokhtar Belmokhtar, a senior leader of AQIM and the organizer of the January 2013 attack on an Algerian gas plant that killed 37 foreigners, including three Americans.[30]

In late August 2013, reports surfaced that a Nigerian JTF spokesman claimed that Nigerian forces had killed Shekau. Despite this initial claim, information corroborating this claim is not yet available. If true, Shekau's death would mark a loss to Boko Haram's short-term planning external communications efforts. However, other senior figures within Boko Haram would likely step forward and prevent the group's collapse.

Mamman Nur

---

[26] "Profile of Nigeria's Boko Haram leader Abubakar Shekau," *BBC News,* June 22, 2012. Available at: http://www.bbc.co.uk/news/world-africa-18020349.
[27] Ibid.
[28] "Terrorist Designations of Boko Haram Commander Abubakar Shekau, Khalid al-Barnawi and Abubakar Adam Kambar," Office of the Spokesperson, *U.S. Department of State*, June 21, 2012. Available at: http://www.state.gov/r/pa/prs/ps/2012/06/193574.htm.
[29] "US offers rewards for capture of African militants," *BBC News*, June 4, 2013. Available at: http://www.bbc.co.uk/news/world-africa-22763305.
[30] "US posts $7 million bounty on Boko Haram leader Abubakar Shekau," John Thomas Didymus, *Digital Journal,* June 4, 2013. Available at: http://www.digitaljournal.com/article/351533.

Mamman Nur is said to be a senior figure or possibly rival leader to Shekau within Boko Haram, and a potential source of internal division.[31,32] Nur, reportedly a native of Nigeria's neighbor Chad, has been described as Boko Haram's third-in-command during its 2009 uprising in northern Nigeria. After the revolt was put down by a brutal military assault he reportedly fled to Somalia to train with al-Shabaab and returned to Nigeria in 2011.[33] Nur also allegedly served as Boko Haram's leader while Shekau recovered from wounds suffered during the 2009 uprising.[34]

At least one local Nigerian account suggests that Nur is a rival to Shekau, noting that Nur and his supporters believe he is better qualified to control Boko Haram because of his exposure to Somali training and contacts.[35] According to some sources, Nur is the brains behind the U.N. facility bombing, making him responsible for the most significant and widely known Boko Haram operation since the group's transformation.[36] On September 18, 2012, the government of Nigeria issued a bounty of $175,000 for Nur, which remains unclaimed.[37] One of many periodic reports of peace talks between the Nigerian government and representatives of Boko Haram notes that Mamman Nur was selected by Shekau to negotiate, indicating perhaps the two are more united than has been otherwise suggested.[38] However, some believe Nur's foreign training and connections have caused a division between Nur and Shekau. As a result, there are indications that Nur's followers have an increasing international focus, and that Ansaru is becoming the more internationally oriented branch of Boko Haram.

Abubakar Adam Kambar and Khalid al-Barnawi

In June 2012, the United States designated Shekau, Abubakar Adam Kambar, and Khalid al-Barnawi, three men associated with Boko Haram, "as specially designated global terrorists under section 1(b) of Executive Order 13224."[39] Kambar and al-Barnawi were also cited for their relationships with other pan-African terror groups such as AQIM.[40] Both are believed to have trained with AQIM in Algeria. This might mean they represent a group of Boko Haram members who have spent time in North Africa with other extremist groups and may be more focused on an international jihadi agenda.

---

[31] "How Nur, Shekau run Boko Haram," Uduma Kalu, *Vanguard,* September 3, 2011. Available at: http://www.vanguardngr.com/2011/09/how-nur-shekau-run-boko-haram/.
[32] "Boko Haram's Evolving Threat," J. Peter Pham, *Africa Security Brief,* April 2012. Available at: http://www.ndu.edu/press/lib/pdf/Africa-Security-Brief/ASB-20.pdf.
[33] "Ansaru: A Profile of Nigeria's Newest Jihadist Movement," *Jamestown Foundation,* January 20, 2013. Available at: http://www.refworld.org/docid/50f69aaf2.html
[34] Kalu, *supra* note 31.
[35] Ibid.
[36] Ibid.
[37] "Nigeria Sets $175,000 Bounty For Mamman Nur, The Alleged UN Office Bomber," *Sahara Reporters,* September 18, 2012. Available at: http://saharareporters.com/news-page/nigeria-sets-175000-bounty-mamman-nur-alleged-un-office-bomber
[38] "Nigeria: FG/Boko Haram - A New Peace Deal?" Vincent Obia, *THISDAY,* November 11, 2012. Available at: http://allafrica.com/stories/201211110303.html?viewall=1.
[39] "US Lists Boko Haram Leaders as Foreign Terrorists." Abiodun Oluwarotimi and George Agba, *Leadership,* June 22, 2012. Available at: http://leadership.ng/nga/articles/27945/2012/06/22/us_lists_boko_haram_leaders_foreign_terrorists.html.
[40] Ibid.

In June 2013, it was revealed that Kambar had been suspected dead for almost a year.[41] It is believed that he was in his mid-30s at the time of his death and a native of the Borno state, which is located in Northern Nigeria. One Nigerian Lieutenant Colonel described Kambar as the key link between AQIM and al-Shabaab.[42]

Khalid al-Barnawi is currently believed to be the most substantial connection between AQIM and Boko Haram, with some suggesting that the adoption of AQIM strategies, such as kidnapping and targeting internationals, can be directly linked to al-Barnawi.[43] Like Kambar, al-Barnawi is believed to be from Borno, or neighboring Niger, and in his mid-30s. It is alleged that following the police battle in 2009, al-Barnawi fled Nigeria and was trained by AQIM. Not only is he currently a suspected member of Boko Haram's Shura Council, but he is also expected to have been an integral part of the international kidnappings that have recently increased in frequency. Some suspect that AQIM paid Boko Haram to abduct foreigners, and that al-Barnawi acts as a major contact between the two groups.[44] Currently, it is thought that he is more closely linked to the Boko Haram splinter group Ansaru.[45] He is also believed to have a relationship with former AQIM leader Mokhtar Belmokhtar that dates back to the mid-2000s. The close links between AQIM, Boko Haram, and Ansaru make al-Barnawi a very dangerous and influential player in West African terrorism.

Internal Divisions

Speaking broadly, Boko Haram faces internal divisions in its own ranks, and has lashed out against dissent within the Nigerian Muslim community. While most of the religiously affiliated targets and casualties of these attacks have been Christian, the majority of Boko Haram's victim's have been northern Nigerian Muslims, and there have been several attacks by the group's members against prominent Muslims (and even reports of members killed for internal disagreements). The group has also attacked mosques – in August 2013, gunmen killed more than 40 people in a Borno state mosque – likely in an effort to warn the population against cooperating with security forces. Boko Haram is believed to be responsible for murdering Sheikh Ibrahim Birkuti, a prominent cleric who had publicly criticized Boko Haram for the spread of violence throughout northern Nigeria.[46] Sheikh Birkuti was killed as he departed a mosque in Biu, south of Maiduguri. Boko Haram has also killed a number of other prominent Muslim leaders, including: "Bashir Kashara, a well-known Wahhabi cleric, killed in October 2010; and Ibrahim Ahmad Abdullahi, a non-violent preacher, killed in June 2011."[47] Members of

---

[41] "JTF claims 'global terrorist' Kabar killed." *Vanguard,* June 07, 2013. Available at: http://www.vanguardngr.com/2013/06/jtf-claims-global-terrorist-kambar-killed/.

[42] Ibid.

[43] "A Brief Look at Ansaru's Khalid al-Barnawi – AQIM's Bridge into Northern Nigeria." Jacob Zenn, *Jamestown Foundation,* March 27, 2013. Available at: http://mlm.jamestown.org/single/?tx_ttnews[tt_news]=40648&tx_ttnews[backPid]=539&cHash=5e9e96a1 3c0613f0c099e10ce70f5eaa#.UfaG5ayobts.

[44] Ibid.

[45] Ibid.

[46] "Boko Haram gunmen kill Nigerian Muslim cleric Birkuti," *BBC News,* June 7, 2012. Available at: http://www.bbc.co.uk/news/world-africa-13679234.

[47] Forest, *supra* note 20, at 68.

the group are also reportedly responsible for killing the brother of one of the most important traditional Islamic rulers in northeast Nigeria, the Shehu of Borno.[48]

Inside the organization, the exact nature of different factions becomes difficult to determine. According to former General Carter F. Ham of U.S. Africa Command (AFRICOM), although Boko Haram as a whole is not a new organization, it contains an evolving element that is far more extreme and growing in strength.[49] Knowledge of some degree of division within Boko Haram has been widespread for some time. Other than Ansaru (addressed below), it is still not yet completely clear that competing factions within the organization distinguish themselves beyond leadership disputes, or whether they view themselves as competing groups. Nonetheless, disagreements among some Boko Haram members are certainly occurring, making the organization more complex and their actions more challenging to predict.

According to the *Associated Press*, in 2011 "one representative of [Boko Haram's] moderate faction was killed after negotiating with former Nigerian President Olusegun Obasanjo."[50] The victim was reportedly a former brother-in-law of Mohammed Yusuf, and had released a statement outlining three conditions for peace: "the rebuilding of their mosque, which had been demolished during the 2009 riots; the payment of compensation to his family as ordered by the court over the extra-judicial killing of their father, Yusuf's father-in-law; and the directive that the security agencies should desist from further harassment of the sect members."[51] Clearly Boko Haram, like all other al Qaeda-affiliated groups, is eager to kill Muslims who stand in their way.

There is also significant evidence that some of the internal divisions within Boko Haram result from tensions between the number of different ethnic groups in the organization's ranks. Boko Haram has expanded its area of operations beyond its traditional stronghold, northeastern Nigeria.[52] However, this expansion has spread across an historical ethno-sectarian fault line. As previously mentioned, the Kanuri people, who comprise a majority of Boko Haram, dominate the northeast state of Borno, but the rest of northern Nigeria is populated in large part by the Hausa-Fulani people. These ethnic groups practice Islam somewhat differently from one another, creating potential tensions. According to one report from STRATFOR Global Intelligence, "As Boko Haram attacks began to kill more Hausa-Fulani, a backlash among western Nigerian Muslims has been mounting, particularly in Kano, Kano state, Nigeria's second largest city and the country's northern commercial hub."[53]

Because of the decentralized nature of Boko Haram's structure, it is open to frequent cases of miscommunication, dissent, and conflicting messaging. In turn, it is likely that these internal problems for Boko Haram only cause further fracturing.

In January 2012 a group claiming to be a moderate breakaway faction of Boko Haram sent a tape to the Nigerian TV channel the National Television Authority, saying

---

[48] BBC News, *supra* note 26.

[49] "African Security Issues," General Carter Ham, Commander, United States Africa Command, June 26, 2012. Available at: http://www.africom.mil/getarticle.asp?art=8039.

[50] "Nigeria: Radical Muslim Sect Grows More Dangerous," Jon Gambrell, *Associated Press,* November 4, 2011. Available at: http://www.breitbart.com/article.php?id=D9QQ3V200&show_article=1.

[51] Forest, *supra* note 20, at 85.

[52] "Boko Haram Faces Backlash in Nigeria," Scott Stewart, *STRATFOR Global Intelligence,* July 2, 2012. Available at: http://www.stratfor.com/analysis/boko-haram-faces-backlash-nigeria.

[53] Ibid.

they were ready to negotiate.[54] Four days later, men claiming to be Boko Haram publicly beheaded six people in Maiduguri. According to the U.S. Institute of Peace, "when Boko Haram kills their own, they behead them, and reports of beheadings seem to go up when there are talks of negotiation."[55] It is plausible that many of these beheadings, which rose in frequency in early 2012, are purges of moderate members who have complained or attempted to negotiate, indicating that Boko Haram's membership may be growing more extreme.[56]

In early February 2012, Nigerian security forces captured Abu Qaqa, the nom de guerre of the designated spokesman for Boko Haram.[57] During questioning, Qaqa hinted of a division within the sect, following continuous arrests of non-Kanuri members (Hausa, Fulani, Chadians, and Nigerians) of Boko Haram. Abu Qaqa reportedly told his interrogators that the arrest of minority ethnicity members sparked mistrust in the ranks:

> *Before I was arrested, some of us were already showing signs of tiredness. Most of us were tired of fighting, but we couldn't come out to say so because of fear of reprisal from leader Imam Shekau on dissenting members. Several of our members who denounced the violent struggle were slaughtered in front of their wives and children. Seven were killed recently. Besides some of us, the non-Kanuri in the sect were worried at the trend of arrests of our members. It is either that the security agents were so good at their job or some of our members were moles giving us out. The worrying aspect was that most of our key members arrested were non-Kanuri, which raised fears that there's sectional betrayal of members.[58]*

In his report released by the Joint Special Operations University, James Forest described the divisions by noting, "some local observers now discriminate between a Kogi Boko Haram, Kanuri Boko Haram, and Hausa Fulani Boko Haram."[59] It is unclear exactly how powerful these ethnic tensions are; yet it would appear unlikely that tribal identities would force Boko Haram to disintegrate. However, divisions over tactics and ideology may have a more direct effect on the group's dynamics.

Ansaru

At least one faction within Boko Haram has managed to distinguish itself by name from the core network, to some degree. The formation of *Jama'atu Ansarul Musilimina fi Biladis Sudan*, more widely known simply as "Ansaru," was publicly announced in January 2012, and was likely the result of growing internal tensions and

---

[54] Walker, *supra* note 23, at 11.

[55] Ibid.

[56] Walker, *supra* note 23, at 6.

[57] "Suspect gives SSS Boko Haram operations clues," Yusuf Alli, *The Nation*, February 7, 2012. Available at: http://www.thenationonlineng net/2011/index.php/news/35982-suspect-gives-sss-boko-haram-operations-clues html.

[58] Ibid.

[59] Forest, *supra* note 23, at 3.

disagreements over leadership style and operations.[60] Abu Usamatul al-Ansari, who many suspect is an alias for Khalid al-Barnawi, is the leader of Ansaru.[61] It has been reported that Ansaru may be more directly focused on targeting Nigerian government facilities and personnel, as opposed to churches, but the group itself issued a rather public repudiation of that theory. It is commonly held that Ansaru has more of an international focus, with the ultimate goal of establishing an Islamic caliphate throughout West Africa, and not just in Nigeria.[62] On June 1, 2012, the Nigerian newspaper *Desert Herald* uploaded two exclusively received videos proclaiming the existence of Ansaru.[63] In the videos, they claimed a different understanding of Jihad and vowed to avenge the killing of Muslims. An initial translation posted by *Desert Herald* reported that Ansaru does not target non-Muslims except "in self-defense or if they attack Muslims like the cases we have in Jos," referring to the indiscriminate killing of Muslims over the summer of 2012.[64] Specifically, they claimed, "Islam forbids the killing of innocent people including non-Muslims. This is our belief and we stand for it."[65]

However, just three days after the videos were released, a self-proclaimed Ansaru spokesman, Abu Ja'afar, sent an email correcting the newspaper's translation of the videos, asserting that the group's original message had been distorted.[66] Particularly, Ja'afar stated:

> *The security officials and the Christians are enemies of Islam and Muslims; therefore we will find them, fight them and kill them whenever we have the chance. We are helpers of Islam and Muslims; we did not mention the phrase: Islam forbids killing of innocent people including non-Muslims. Killing them is part of Jihad. We will target and kill any security personnel who is under the [Nigerian] constitution and those among us why by any means protect infidels.[67]*

Of course, whether embracing or disowning the murder of non-Muslims, Ansaru nonetheless utilizes terrorist activity to wage jihad. According to the email, "The word of 'Jihad,' as clarified by Allah involves all that one may use to upraise, support or defend the religion of truth and bring down the injustice and infidelity, either with knowledge,

---

[60] "Rift in Boko Haram, 'Ansaru' Splinter Group Emerges, Calls BH 'Inhuman' To Muslims," *SaharaReporters*, January 31, 2012. Available at: http://saharareporters.com/news-page/rift-boko-haram-'ansaru'-splinter-group-emerges-calls-bh-'inhuman'-muslims.

[61] "Nigeria's New Face of Terror." *PMNews*, February 26, 2013. Available at: http://pmnewsnigeria.com/2013/02/26/nigerias-new-face-of-terror/

[62] "Abu Usmatal al-Ansari Announces Boko Haram Breakaway Faction," *Jamestown Foundation*, June 30 2012. Available at: http://mlm.jamestown.org/single/?tx_ttnews[tt_news]=39564&tx_ttnews[backPid]=539&cHash=268f317c 28e5f58115c512c17f744bd8#.UfbLkayobts

[63] "Nigerian Jihadist Group Declares Founding in Statement," SITE Monitoring Service, July 09, 2012, pg. 1.

[64] "New Islamist group emerges in Nigeria, claims 'different' understanding of Jihad," Eman El-Shenawi, *Al-Arabiya*, June 3, 2012. Available at: http://www.alarabiya net/articles/2012/06/03/218371.html.

[65] Ibid.

[66] "Latest: Security Official and Christians are enemies of Islam and Muslims, we will target and kill them-Says Spokesman of Jama'atu Ansarul Muslimina fi Biladi Sudan, Abu Ja'afar," *Desert Herald*, June 5, 2012. Available at: http://desertherald.com/?p=1582.

[67] Ibid.

weapons or properties."[68] This leaves Ansaru significant room to maneuver and suggests that they are committed to armed operations.

Ansaru's presence has been known publicly in Nigeria since late January 2012.[69] Shortly after Boko Haram's January 26, 2012 attacks in Kano that killed over 200 people, fliers were disseminated throughout the city introducing this new organization. The fliers were signed by Abu Usamatul Ansari, the self-proclaimed leader of Ansaru, and stated the group's motto, "fighting and sacrificing for Allah's cause."[70] This confirms Ansaru's presence in Kano a full four months before their video debut. As of yet, the numerical and tactical strength of Ansaru is still unknown, as is the true identity of its leadership. However, the videos were released in Arabic, English, and Hausa.[71] While many in Nigeria speak English (the country's official language), it is possible to imagine that the release of Ansaru's announcement in international languages such as Arabic and English may also be an appeal to a wider audience of supporters outside of Nigeria. If this were true, between Ansaru and the wider Boko Haram network – still relatively vague to outside observers – may actually be Ansaru's more direct embrace of international jihadist support.

On November 22, 2012, the Home Office of the United Kingdom listed Ansaru as a Proscribed Terrorist Organization (PTO), which made "membership of, and support for, the organization a criminal offence."[72] The designation of Ansaru as a PTO was tied to the group's reported involvement in the May 2011 kidnapping and subsequent March 2012 murder of a British citizen. In the 2012 Country Report on Terrorism, the State Department noted that, "of particular concern to the United States is the emergence of the BH faction known as 'Ansaru,' which has close ties to AQIM and has prioritized targeting Westerners – including Americans – in Nigeria."[73]

It is certainly possible that Ansaru may prove itself an entirely independent and perhaps even more dangerous terrorist threat. Both Boko Haram and Ansaru appear to be aligned with al Qaeda's objectives and have some mutual history with one another. For the moment, they contribute to the violence in Nigeria and elsewhere and cannot be ignored or viewed in a vacuum. It is important that we learn more about both groups, and take steps to eradicate the threat. Toward that end, the threat from Ansaru should also be considered in any U.S. effort to assist Nigeria in dealing with Boko Haram, including FTO designations.

---

[68] Ibid.

[69] "Boko Haram: Splinter Group, Ansaru Emerges," *Vanguard*, February 1, 2012. Available at: http://www.vanguardngr.com/2012/02/boko-haram-splinter-group-ansaru-emerges/

[70] Ibid.

[71] SITE Monitoring Service, *supra* note 63.

[72] "Britain bans Nigerian Islamist group accused of murder," *Reuters,* November 22, 2012. Available at: http://articles.chicagotribune.com/2012-11-22/news/sns-rt-us-britain-nigeria-islamistsbre8al0vn-20121122_1_nigerian-islamist-mcmanus-and-lamolinara-franco-lamolinara.

[73] "Country Reports on Terrorism 2012," *The U.S. Department of State*, May 30 2013. Available at: http://www.state.gov/j/ct/rls/crt/2012/209979.htm.

II.

Continued Evolution

Increasing Operational Capability

A number of trends have emerged from Boko Haram's claimed attacks, each demonstrating increasing capabilities and sophistication. According a June 2012 report on Nigeria issued by the Congressional Research Service, "Boko Haram's attacks have increased substantially in frequency, reach, and lethality, now occurring almost daily in northeast Nigeria, and periodically beyond."[74] As detailed later on, they may have also taken steps to penetrate Nigerian security forces. If true, that level of sophistication is an indication that the group continues to further mature their operational savvy, and expand their threat.

There has also been an increase in the group's use of suicide bombings.[75] As of May 14, 2013, Boko Haram engaged in at least sixteen different suicide attacks, according to the Institute for the Study of Violent Groups and Nigerian media reports.[76] These attacks targeted Christian churches, police stations, local newspaper offices, and government buildings. In comparison, between Boko Haram's first suicide attack on June 16, 2011 and December 31, 2011, they conducted only six suicide attacks.[77] This development indicates two things: that the group has attracted a core of recruits willing to die for their cause, and that it possesses the capability to build sophisticated explosives at a rapid pace.

Given the types of attacks they have conducted so far, as well as the explosive devices and components seized by Nigerian security forces, it appears as if Boko Haram has access to a significant amount of explosive material.[78] Boko Haram not only employs improvised explosive devices (IEDs) in its operations, but somehow utilizes commercial explosives as well. One theory on the origin of these explosives, presented by Scott Stewart of STRATFOR Global Intelligence, is that Boko Haram may be obtaining the material from central Nigerian mining operations. This fear was substantiated in July 2013 when suspected Boko Haram operatives raided a Yobe construction site. The operatives arrived in the early morning, overcame the security guards, and fled with 125 kilograms of explosives and hundreds of detonators.[79]

The group also appears to have highly skilled bomb makers, and though the IEDs they deploy are simple in their design, they maintain a high rate of success.[80] According

---

[74] "Nigeria: Current Issues and U.S. Policy," Lauren Ploch, *U.S. Congressional Research Service*, July 18, 2012, pg. 11.

[75] "Boko Haram: An Increasingly Radical Threat," *The Soufan Group*, June 19, 2012. Available at: http://soufangroup.com/briefs/details/?Article_Id=319.

[76] Institute for the Study of Violent Groups. 2012. vkb.isvg.org/ (Accessed July 19, 2012).

[77] "Ibid.

[78] "Nigeria's Boko Haram Militants Remain a Regional Threat," Scott Stewart, *STRATFOR Global Intelligence*, January 26, 2012. Available at: http://www.stratfor.com/weekly/nigerias-boko-haram-militants-remain-regional-threat.

[79] "Suspected Boko Haram Members Steal 125 kg of Dynamite in Yobe." *Daily Times*, July 31, 2013. Available at: http://www.dailytimes.com.ng/article/suspected-boko-haram-members-steal-125-kg-dynamite-yobe

[80] Stewart, *supra* note 78.

to STRATFOR Global Intelligence, bomb making is a process that normally follows a significant learning curve absent outside instruction from a more experienced bomb maker.[81] Boko Haram's proficiency suggests the group's bomb maker(s) indeed received training from experienced militants elsewhere, potentially indicating a stronger relationship between AQIM or al-Shabaab.

Besides *building* sophisticated weaponry, it is now possible that Boko Haram has acquired, or will acquire, SA-7 and SA-24 shoulder-fired surface-to-air missiles.[82] Of 20,000 such weapons in Libya, only 5,000 of them had been secured through a $40 million U.S. program to buy up loose missiles during the fall of the Gadhafi regime.[83] The *Washington Post* reported in early 2012 that two former CIA officers have been raising this issue repeatedly with current law enforcement and intelligence community contacts. In an email, these officers explain, "The missiles and munitions that have been streaming out of Libya since the fall of 2011 have made their way to Agadez in Niger and points west…Boko Haram has taken possession of some of the refurbished missiles. They have brought Egyptian Army ordinance technicians to refurbish and test the SA-7B missiles pictured below…The source claims that some 800 missiles are available in the area."[84]

The SA-7 is effective up to 1,300 meters, while some newer models reach altitudes of almost four kilometers.[85] Reportedly, most commercial aircraft cruise around 9,140 meters, and so remain out of range while inflight. However, the weapons could be used to target aircraft during the takeoff and landing.[86] It is worth noting that two similar missiles were used to shoot down a Rwandan government flight, killing the presidents of Rwanda and Burundi in April 1994. More recently, in 2002, SA-7s were fired at an Israeli jet as it prepared to depart the airport in Mombasa, Kenya.[87] It does not take much imagination to picture the threat these weapons would pose to commercial aviation in Abuja if they fell into Boko Haram's hands. Nothing the organization has done so far gives the impression that they would restrain themselves from hitting aiming for such a target if given the opportunity.

Boko Haram has also shown increasing intent – and no lack of capability – in targeting Western interests. Over the last three years, the U.S. Embassy in Abuja has issued multiple warnings that Boko Haram was planning attacks against Western interests, including against hotels frequented by Western guests.[88] In response to the growing danger, western airlines reportedly stopped allowing flight crewmembers to stay

---

[81] Ibid.

[82] "Libyan missiles on the loose," David Ignatius, *The Washington Post*, May 8, 2012. Available at: http://www.washingtonpost.com/opinions/libyan-missiles-on-the-loose/2012/05/08/gIQA1FCUBU_story.html.

[83] Ibid.

[84] Ibid.

[85] "The Continuing Threat of Libyan Missiles," Scott Stewart, *STRATFOR Global Intelligence*, May 3, 2012. Available at: http://www.stratfor.com/weekly/continuing-threat-libyan-missiles.

[86] Ibid.

[87] "Israel Evacuates Tourists from Kenya," *BBC News*, November 29, 2002. Available at: news.bbc.co.uk/2/hi/Africa/2525931.stm

[88] "Messages for American Citizens," United States Diplomatic Mission to Nigeria. Available at: http://nigeria.usembassy.gov/warden_messages.html.

over in Abuja.[89] After landing in Abuja, crews fly to Lagos or Accra, Ghana to spend the night. According to *The Guardian Nigeria*, "there are indications that one of the United States carriers designated to Abuja is putting finishing touches to stopping its operations to the area because of security reasons..."[90] Meanwhile, according to Nigerian media reports, the group issued a threat in February 2012 that it intended to assassinate the U.S. Ambassador to Nigeria.[91] If Boko Haram were taken at their word, this would mean that the group is targeting U.S. interests and persons.

Al Qaeda in Nigeria

In answers provided to the Senate Armed Services Committee (SASC) in advance of his February 14, 2013 confirmation hearing, General David M. Rodriguez – currently serving as Commander of AFRICOM – named Boko Haram as an al Qaeda affiliate.[92] This is perhaps the most direct assessment of the al Qaeda / Boko Haram relationship issued by a major U.S. official, but is not the first time Boko Haram has been identified as an ally of al Qaeda.

The relationship between al Qaeda in the Islamic Maghreb (AQIM) and Boko Haram is now known and well established, although its exact nature is subject to debate. As early as January 2010, AQIM leader Abdelmalek Droukdel announced that AQIM would assist Boko Haram with training, personnel, and equipment.[93] In November 2011, Boko Haram's official spokesman, Abu Qaqa, stated, "We are together with al Qaeda. They are promoting the cause of Islam just as we are doing. Therefore they help us in our struggle and we help them, too."[94] A senior Nigerian military officer was more blunt, stating in August 2013, that "Boko Haram is al-Qaeda."[95] AQIM providing Boko Haram with advanced training and new techniques poses a significant threat to international security. In exchange for training, AQIM expands its operating space into Nigeria, a country of significant importance to the United States.

The cooperation between AQIM and Boko Haram has been publicly documented, as the Nigerian Foreign Minister Olugbenga Ashiru noted that Boko Haram members

---

[89] "Airlines stop crew's stay in Abuja over insecurity," Francis Obinor and Wole Shadare, *The Guardian Nigeria*, July 5, 2012. Available at:
http://www.ngrguardiannews.com/index.php?option=com_content&view=article&id=91371:airlines-stop-crews-stay-in-abuja-over-insecurity-&catid=1:national&Itemid=559
[90] Ibid.
[91] The Soufan Group, *supra* note 75.
[92] "Advance Policy Questions for General David M. Rodriguez, U.S. Army Nominee for Commander, U. S. Africa Command," General David Rodriguez, United States Senate Committee on Armed Services, February 13, 2013. Available at: http://www.armed-services.senate.gov/statemnt/2013/02%20February/Rodriguez%2002-14-13.pdf.
[93] "Maghrebian Militant Maneuvers: AQIM as a Strategic Challenge," Felipe Pathe Duarte, *Center for Strategic and International Studies*, September 28, 2011. Available at:
http://csis.org/publication/maghrebian-militant-maneuvers-aqim-strategic-challenge.
[94] "Special Report: Boko Haram-between rebellion and jihad," Joe Brock, *Reuters,* January 31, 2012. Available at: http://www.reuters.com/article/2012/01/31/us-nigeria-bokoharam-idUSTRE80U0LR20120131.
[95] "Boko Haram is no African al-Qaeda." Virginia Comolli, *International Institute for Strategic Studies*, 17 August 2012. Available at: http://iissvoicesblog.wordpress.com/2012/08/17/boko-haram-is-no-african-al-qaeda/

have received AQIM training in Mali.[96] As the Subcommittee on Counterterrorism and Intelligence noted in their 2011 report, General Carter Ham, former commander of U.S. Africa Command, confirmed as early as August 2011 that "multiple unnamed sources indicate that Boko Haram had made contact with operatives from AQIM and with the Somali terrorist group Al-Shabaab."[97] In January 2012, Niger's Foreign Minister, Mohamed Bazoum stated, "there is no doubt that there is confirmed information that shows a link between Boko Haram and AQIM, and it consists primarily of the training given to elements of Boko Haram." [98] According to *Reuters*, this account is backed up by sources in Nigeria that claim AQIM – Boko Haram links may go back as far as seven years.[99] Given the evidence detailed throughout this and other reports, it is becoming evident that the relationship between Boko Haram and AQIM is no longer strongly suspected: it is a mature relationship that allows Boko Haram an avenue to advance its capability, and gives AQIM influence over a developing al Qaeda affiliate and a rich target list.

Concerns that Boko Haram was collaborating with al Qaeda came to the forefront following their suicide attacks on police facilities and the U.N. building in Abuja in 2011. This attack marked Boko Haram's second deployment of a suicide bomb and its first attack of global significance.[100] The attack was also far more sophisticated than anything linked to Boko Haram before. It involved the use of at least two different types of manufactured explosives, including pentaerythritol tetranitrate (PETN) and triacetone triperoxide (TATP).[101] According to Sidney Alford, a British explosives expert, "The only form of PETN that is commonly available is the core explosive in detonating cord. You can get detonating cord from the manufacturers, the army, or from blasting contractors in the demolition or quarrying industries."[102] On their own, these elements only lead to speculation about an AQIM-Boko Haram alliance. It is in combination with the organizations' public declarations of support, reports of movements of money, weapons, and personnel, which confirm it.

Since 2011, Boko Haram has gradually made a transition to an increasingly sophisticated terrorist group, aided by AQIM training. The U.N. attack "...has officials and experts worrying that a branch of al-Qaeda has spread its influence to Nigeria, Africa's most populous country and a key supplier of oil for the U.S. and the world market."[103] In early February 2012, *The Daily Telegraph* discussed the evolution of Boko Haram's actions noting, "[Boko Haram] once specialized in robbing banks and attacking defenceless Christian congregations. In the past month however, its gunmen or suicide

---

[96] "Nigeria's Boko Haram Members Trained in Mali, Minister Says," William Davison, Maram Mazen, *Bloomberg*, January 25, 2013. Available at: http://www.bloomberg.com/news/2013-01-25/nigeria-s-boko-haram-members-trained-in-mali-minister-says html.

[97] "Nigeria's Boko Haram: Al-Qaeda's New Friend in Africa?" Karen Leigh, *TIME*, August 31, 2011. Available at: http://www.time.com/time/world/article/0,8599,2091137,00.html.

[98] "Boko Haram got al Qaeda bomb training, Niger says," Laurent Prieur, *Reuters,* January 25, 2012. Available at: http://af reuters.com/article/idAFJOE80O00K20120125.

[99] Brock, *supra* note 94.

[100] "Global Jihad Sustained Through Africa," Valentina Soria, *Royal United Services Institute for Defence and Security Studies,* April 2012, pg. 8. Available at: http://www rusi.org/downloads/assets/UKTA2.pdf.

[101] Brock, *supra* note 94.

[102] Ibid.

[103] Leigh, *supra* note 97.

bombers have struck 21 times, killing at least 253 people."[104] Since the U.N. bombing, Boko Haram has carried out attacks nearly every week, often in public settings and on public buildings.[105]

AQIM training and influence is also reflected in Boko Haram's use of the Internet in order to spread violent messages in a manner similar to many AQ affiliates. A YouTube video released in January 2012 featured Boko Haram leader Abubakar Shekau discussing the state of Nigeria and glorifying Boko Haram's actions against Christians mirrors those made by al-Qaeda leaders in the past. In the video, "his beard, headscarf and hand gestures recall the style of video pronouncements made by the late al Qaeda leader Osama Bin Laden."[106] The video also has familiar jihadist undertones, such as the bulletproof jacket and Kalashnikov rifles prominent in the video shot.[107] This signifies that beyond operational support, a collective spirit of global jihad may be unifying Boko Haram and AQIM.

In addition to training, "[The partnership between AQIM and Boko Haram] can also mean an increase in cash flow for Boko Haram, which currently makes most of its money…by robbing banks throughout the Muslim northern half of the country."[108] The relationship between AQIM and Boko Haram has also influenced the adoption of kidnapping as a source of income, netting the group millions of dollars from ransoms. AQIM is fiscally sound and has an arsenal of weapons at its disposal that has proven useful to Boko Haram.[109]

The first documented kidnapping by Boko Haram appears to have occurred in March 2011, orchestrated by "the Abu Mohammed-led faction of Boko Haram in Nigeria" and resulting in the deaths of two European hostages (and Boko Haram member Abu Mohammed).[110] In January 2012, a German engineer named Edgar Raupach was kidnapped in Nigeria for ransom, and killed in a failed rescue attempt in May.[111] Although Boko Haram has denied any involvement in that kidnapping, some analysts, such as Martin Ewi from South Africa's Institute for Security Studies, believe that Boko Haram aided AQIM in Raupach's abduction in return for the training they received from AQIM.[112] The 2013 abduction of a French family of seven in Cameroon is a continuance of the pattern of targeting Westerners.

---

[104] "Al-Qaeda's hand in Boko Haram's deadly Nigerian attacks," David Blair, *The Daily Telegraph,* February 5, 2012. Available at: http://www.telegraph.co.uk/news/worldnews/al-qaeda/9062825/Al-Qaedas-hand-in-Boko-Harams-deadly-Nigerian-attacks.html.

[105] Walker, *supra* note 23, at 1.

[106] Brock, *supra* note 94.

[107] Ibid.

[108] Leigh, *supra* note 97.

[109] Ibid.

[110] "Nigerian 'mastermind' of British and Italian Hostage Kidnap Dies," Christopher McManus, *The Telegraph,* March 14, 2012. Available at: http://www.telegraph.co.uk/news/worldnews/africaandindianocean/nigeria/9144417/Nigerian-mastermind-of-British-and-Italian-hostage-kidnap-dies.html.

[111] "Abducted German engineer 'killed in Nigeria'," *BBC News*, May 31, 2012. Available at: http://www.bbc.co.uk/news/world-africa-18278740.

[112] "Kidnapping Shows 2 Terror Groups in North Nigeria," *Associated Press,* March 24, 2012. Available at: http://www.foxnews.com/world/2012/03/24/kidnapping-shows-2-terror-groups-in-north-nigeria/.

Additionally, the instability in Mali allowed AQIM a relatively unencumbered area of operations wherein they trained Boko Haram members.[113] In 2013, it was reported that AQIM organized training facilities on the outskirts of Timbuktu, with over 200 Nigerians in attendance in April 2012. At these facilities, Boko Haram militants reportedly learned tactical skills, such as how to operate unspecified crew serve weapons.[114] The reported massive influx of weapons from northern Mali and the increasingly positive relationship between Boko Haram and AQIM are additional concerns.[115] In 2012, Boko Haram reportedly participated in the attack on the Algerian consulate in Gao, Northern Mali. Abu Sidibe, a regional deputy, noted that there were a hundred Boko Haram members in Gao at the time.[116] It appears that Boko Haram has allowed AQIM members a certain degree of influence within Nigeria, and perhaps that certain elements of Boko Haram are even submitting to a command-control relationship with that wing of al Qaeda. There is speculation that the foreign kidnappings perpetrated by Boko Haram were directly requested or influenced by AQIM.[117] Following the brazen and direct attack against the U.S. facility in Benghazi, Libya that killed four people, AQIM's reach into Nigeria should be viewed as threatening to our diplomatic posts throughout the country. As noted above, the U.S. Embassy in Abuja has *already* issued multiple warnings about threats to American citizens in Nigeria. The danger that Boko Haram may try a similar assault on diplomatic personnel there, as they did in Libya, is a terrifying possibility.

Draining the Nigerian State

For the United States, the strength and viability of a major regional ally and source of oil is a serious concern. From their uprising in 2009 to their current string of attacks, the devastation that Boko Haram inflicts upon Nigeria has persistently grown at an alarming rate. According to Human Rights Watch, more than 3,000 people have fallen victim to Boko Haram's terrorist attacks since mid-2009.[118] In the first ten months of 2012, the deaths of over 900 additional people were blamed on Boko Haram which is, according to Human Rights Watch, "more than in 2010 and 2011 combined."[119]

---

[113] "Mali Islamist Rebels Say 18.4 Million Ransom Paid, Prisoners Released to Free 3 Europeans," *Associated Press*, July 20, 2012. Available at: http://www.washingtonpost.com/world/africa/mali-islamist-rebels-say-184-million-ransom-paid-prisoners-released-to-free-3-europeans/2012/07/20/gJQA1dnkxW_print.html.

[114] "Nigeria: Boko Haram Training Camps Found in Mali." Habeeb I. Pindiga, *Daily Trust,* 6 February 2013. Available at: http://allafrica.com/stories/201302060749 html

[115] Ibid.

[116] "Dozens of Boko Haram Help Mali's rebels seize Gao." *Vanguard*, 9 April 2012. Available at: http://www.vanguardngr.com/2012/04/dozens-of-boko-haram-help-malis-rebel-seize-gao/

[117] "Boko Haram's Evolving Tactics and Alliances in Nigeria." Jacob Zenn, *Combatting Terrorism Center,* June 25, 2013. Available at: http://www.ctc.usma.edu/posts/boko-harams-evolving-tactics-and-alliances-in-nigeria

[118] "Letter to the Committee on Dialogue and Peaceful Resolution of Security Challenges in the North." Daniel Bekele and Richard Dicker, *Human Rights Watch*, June 24 2013. Available at: http://www.hrw.org/node/116887

[119] "World Report: Nigeria." *Human Rights Watch,* 2013. Available at: http://www.hrw.org/world-report/2013/country-chapters/nigeria

It has been the stated political agenda of Boko Haram to turn Nigeria into an Islamic state governed solely by a strict interpretation and implementation of Sharia law.[120] Although it appears highly unlikely Boko Haram could successfully overthrow the current democratically elected government of Nigeria's President Goodluck Jonathan outright, it would be a huge mistake for the U.S. Intelligence Community to dismiss or underestimate Boko Haram as just another regional anti-government grassroots movement. Aside from the ceaseless attacks carried out by Boko Haram, the retaliations by the Nigerian police and military, as well as the State Security Service (SSS), in the forms of excessive violence and human rights abuses, all serve to weaken the Nigerian government and further inflame the Nigeria's domestic tensions. In order to understand this conflict, the aggravations and grievances at the root of northern distrust for their government must be thoroughly and carefully examined.

From Boko Haram's inception, and through the stewardship of its former leader Mohammed Yusuf up until 2009, the largest operation carried out by the group involved intermittent skirmishes on government facilities and police stations in 2004.[121] Yet today, according to former U.S. Assistant Secretary of State for African Affairs Johnnie Carson, "Boko Haram has created widespread insecurity across northern Nigeria, increased tensions between various ethnic communities, interrupted development activities, frightened off investors, and generated concerns among Nigeria's northern neighbors."[122] Through these activities, it is the goal of Boko Haram "to humiliate and undermine the government and to exploit religious differences in order to create chaos and to make Nigeria ungovernable."[123]

This continual degradation of the quality of life in northern Nigeria – already quite low – weakens the state's legitimacy in the eyes of its citizens. But it is not merely poverty and corruption that play a role. Nigeria's law enforcement and military forces attempting to eradicate Boko Haram have very likely engaged in atrocious human rights abuses, even as they fight the ruthless and bloody Boko Haram. Fighting between Nigeria's Joint Task Force and Boko Haram members in the northern town of Baga in April 2013, for example, reportedly resulted in the destruction of homes and the death of more than 180 people, many of whom were believed to be civilians.[124] Several Nigeria experts have cautioned "that the Nigerian government's own response to Boko Haram has been, to date, heavy-handed and may actually fuel radical recruitment."[125] For example, shortly after the Kano church bombings of January 2012, many northern Nigerians were quick to blame the Nigerian government instead of Boko Haram. Many people gathered to channel "their heated discontent, not with Boko Haram, but with what they describe[d] as a shared enemy: the Nigerian state, seen by the poor as a purveyor of

---

[120] "Terrorism in Nigeria: the Rise of Boko Haram," Christopher Bartolotta, *World Policy Journal,* September 19, 2011. Available at: http://www.worldpolicy.org/blog/2011/09/19/terrorism-nigeria-rise-boko-haram.

[121] "To Be Or Not To Be: Is Boko Haram a Foreign Terrorist Organization?" Shannon Connell, *Global Security Studies,* pg. 88. Available at: http://globalsecuritystudies.com/Connell%20Boko%20Haram.pdf.

[122] "Nigeria, One Year After Elections," Johnnie Carson, Assistant Secretary of State for African Affairs, April 9, 2012. Available at: http://www.state.gov/p/af/rls/rm/2012/187721 htm.

[123] Ibid.

[124] "Nigeria: Massive Destruction, Deaths From Military Raid," *Human Rights Watch,* May 1, 2013. Available at: https://www.hrw.org/news/2013/05/01/nigeria-massive-destruction-deaths-military-raid

[125] Ploch, *supra* note 74, at 12.

inequality."[126] Northern Nigerians cite the country's pervasive poverty, injustice, and a general sense of disinterest from their politicians as reasons why they feel their government has cheated them.[127] On April 25, 2012, Principal Deputy Assistant Secretary of State for African Affairs Don Yamamoto, currently serving as acting Assistant Secretary of State for African Affairs, addressed these concerns at a House of Representatives Foreign Affairs Committee hearing and warned the Nigerian government, "Heavy-handed tactics and extrajudicial killings reinforce northerners' concerns that the Nigerian government does not care about them."[128] It is quite clear, given these concerns, that the Nigerian government should be putting greater emphasis on the professionalization of its police and armed forces and prosecuting abuses carried out by its own forces.[129]

In addition, retaliatory attacks by Christian groups in Nigeria will only serve to prolong the crisis, and further stress the resources of the Nigerian government as it attempts to keep the peace. With the reemergence of Boko Haram in the early part of 2010, the frequency and magnitude of the group's attacks have not only escalated, but the tactics and targets have shifted as well. According to a Boko Haram spokesman, the church bombings serve as revenge for "previous Christian 'atrocities' against Muslims."[130] Ultimately, it appears to be the objective of Boko Haram to see that the church bombings are enough to threaten the overall stability of Nigeria and create a greater rift in the religious divisions between the Muslims and Christians of Nigeria.

Not surprisingly, the Boko Haram attacks on churches have not been a one-sided conflict and have prompted Christian reprisals. For example, shortly after the bombings of three churches in June 2012, riots broke out across Kaduna as Christian youths took their anger out to the streets and began attacking Muslims.[131] As attacks on Christians escalate, it is becoming more common for Christian leaders, such as Pastor Ayo Oritsejafor, to suggest the need for Nigerian Christians to begin arming themselves in self-defense.[132] This has raised serious concerns that the bombings conducted by Boko Haram are also intended to provoke altercation on the part of Christians as a means to not only further inflame local religious tensions, but to broadcast their mission around the Muslim world, perhaps in an attempt to paint themselves as a "legitimate" Muslim force defending themselves against infidels. Nigeria must not fall into this trap.

Aside from the religious divisions in Nigeria, which distinguishes the Muslim north from the Christian south, economics also plays a pivotal role. Oil, which makes up roughly 80% of Nigeria's annual revenues, contributes to the tension between north and

---

[126] "In Nigeria, a Deadly Group's Rage Has Local Roots," Adam Nossiter, *the New York Times,* February 25, 2012. Available at: http://www.nytimes.com/2012/02/26/world/africa/in-northern-nigeria-boko-haram-stirs-fear-and-sympathy html?pagewanted=all.

[127] Ibid.

[128] "For African Anti-Terrorism, Region Must Lead, but U.S. Is Helping," Stephen Kaufman, *U.S. Africa Command*, April 26, 2012. Available at: http://www.africom mil/getArticle.asp?art=7839&lang=0.

[129] Ibid.

[130] "Nigeria's Boko Haram 'bombed Kaduna churches," *BBC News*, June 18, 2012. Available at: http://www.bbc.co.uk/news/world-africa-18496285.

[131] Ibid.

[132] "Linkages Between Boko Haram and al Qaeda: A Potential Deadly Synergy," Sean M. Gourley, *Global Security Studies*, Summer 2012. Available at: http://globalsecuritystudies.com/Gourley%20Boko%20Haram.pdf.

south.[133] Geographically, the comparatively more prosperous, oil-rich, largely Christian populated area of southern Nigeria has proven to be economically healthier in comparison to the poverty-stricken, and predominantly Muslim north. Nigeria currently produces an average of about 2.4 million barrels per day, thus making it Africa's largest producer of oil and one of the top oil exporters to the United States.[134] There is concern that Boko Haram may increasingly target Nigeria's oil capabilities as a symbol of the disparities between the North and South. In May 2013, the group targeted the former Minister of Petroleum and held him for ransom for several days, establishing a troubling precedent.[135] In addition, the Niger Delta, located in the southernmost region of the country, accounts for over 75% of the oil produced in Nigeria.[136] Despite the immense wealth generated by this industry, major sections of northern Nigeria remain hugely undeveloped. Corruption appears to be entirely pervasive throughout the Nigerian system, and many northern Nigerian political leaders feel they have been slighted by the Jonathan regime.

Boko Haram's threat to the southern oil sector presents significant risks. The southern Christian group Movement for the Emancipation of the Niger Delta (MEND) has issued a warning of response if Boko Haram or its affiliates attack the oil sector. A violent response from MEND risks a civil war between North and South, which could serve as an opportunity for Boko Haram to train future terrorists, strengthen the conviction of current fighters, and widen the instability.[137]

Many of these conditions pre-date Boko Haram, and Boko Haram's existence and agenda are tangential to these problems. Yet, it is true that the continuing failure of the Nigerian government to address these and other critical issues satisfactorily contributes to general mistrust among its people. Though Boko Haram cannot solve these crises, they are reaping the benefits of a frustrated, disillusioned population. Jobless, angry young men form a massive talent pool from which Boko Haram can draw, while broader northern society somewhat justifiably views the federal government and security services trying to eradicate Boko Haram with contempt. Therefore, while it should not be misunderstood that Boko Haram serves, represents, or fights for Nigeria's poor northern population – such an assertion is an insult to northern Nigerians – it is absolutely essential to note that the systemic failure of the Nigerian government to provide reasonable services to its people or even to police them responsibly only makes matters worse.

Nigerian Counter Offensive

In May 2013, Nigerian President Goodluck Jonathon declared a state of emergency in the three northern states of Yobe, Borno, and Adamawa, the strongholds

---

[133] Ploch, *supra* note 74, at 5.

[134] Ibid.

[135] "Boko Haram Releases Abducted Former Nigeria Oil Minister, 92," *Africa Review*, May 6 2013. Available at: http://www.africareview.com/News/Boko-Haram-releases-abducted-former-oil-minister/-/979180/1843966/-/embjwe/-/index.html

[136] Ploch, *supra* note 74, at 5.

[137] Nigeria Christians Threaten Religious War," *United Press International,* April 23, 2013. Available at: http://www.upi.com/Top_News/Special/2013/04/23/Nigeria-Christians-threaten-religious-war/UPI-73101366742735/

for Boko Haram within Nigeria. The government initially attempted to make amends with the release of certain Boko Haram prisoners, and talk of potential amnesty.[138] Around this time the government also began to encourage the establishment of Civilian Joint Task Forces (CJTF), which served as vigilante groups with the goal of rooting out members of Boko Haram. After the initial public appeals for reconciliation proved futile, a full counter offensive began. In a major show of force, Boko Haram attacked a Yobe secondary school on July 7th, 2013. A Boko Haram spokesman reportedly claimed the attacks were a response to a recent incident at a Koranic school where Muslim pupils were beaten by Nigerian soldiers.[139] Two days later, rumors surfaced that a ceasefire had been signed, and Boko Haram leaders had begged the country for forgiveness. These rumors were dispelled four days later when Shekau said that he would not, "enter a truce with these infidels."[140]

The three states in question have become increasingly violent. A recent major attack on July 26, 2013 occurred in the cities of Mainok and Dawashi in Borno after the CJTF entered searching for Boko Haram militants. The CJTF were fired upon by the militants, and the ensuing firefight resulted in twenty civilian deaths.[141] On the same day, the CJTF had made some arrests and were ambushed while taking the prisoners to the state capital. In retaliation for the attempted arrests, Boko Haram attacked the nearest village under suspicion that it housed those responsible.[142]

In August 2013, the counteroffensive saw a southward movement of Boko Haram members. One Nigerian senator claimed that Boko Haram was moving southwest into Lagos and Ogun and that the group still maintained a force of over six thousand.[143] If true, the movement south could lead to increased conflict with MEND, or Boko Haram could continue to flow outside of Nigerian borders, increasing the international fallout from the conflict.

While it is still unclear whether President Jonathan's efforts will succeed in destroying Boko Haram, history shows that his strategy may further weaken stability in the country if the vigilante forces promote more violence and drive more northerners towards Boko Haram. There have been reports of human rights abuses by the military, police, and vigilante forces. The practices of extrajudicial killings and creation of battlegrounds on the streets will further antagonize the northern population. The danger of a civil war between the north and the south must be avoided. There are also concerns that even if Jonathan's strategy is successful, the movement could survive and be pushed into Cameroon and Niger instead of Nigeria, due to porous borders and Boko Haram's

---

[138] "Nigeria to free Boko Haram Members," Al-Jazeera, 21 May 2013. Available at:
http://www.aljazeera.com/news/africa/2013/05/201352117343462308.html
[139] "Extremists Attack in Nigeria Kills 42 at Boarding School," Damien McElroy, *The Telegraph*, July 06, 2013. Available at:
http://www.telegraph.co.uk/news/worldnews/africaandindianocean/nigeria/10163942/Extremist-attack-in-Nigeria-kills-42-at-boarding-school.html.
[140] "Nigeria: Boko Harm Denies Cease-Fire, Explains Yobe School Massacre," Tony Nwankwo, *Vanguard*, 14 July 2013. Available at: http://allafrica.com/stories/201307151412.html.
[141] "Nigeria: Boko Haram Kills 43 Borno Villagers," Hamza Idris, *Daily Trust,* 29 July 2013. Available at: http://allafrica.com/stories/201307291041.html?viewall=1.
[142] Ibid.
[143] "Nigeria: 35 Killed in Borno As Boko Haram Attack Security Formations," Ola' Audu, *Premium Times,* August 5, 2013. Available at: http://allafrica.com/stories/201308060669.html

existing networks in those regions.[144] Additionally, Ansaru, the more radical branch, could become an even greater worldwide threat, in a parallel to al-Shabaab's emergence after the fall of the Islamic Courts Union in Somalia.

---

[144] "Boko Haram is no African al-Qaeda." Virginia Comolli, *International Institute for Strategic Studies,* 17 August 2012. Available at: http://iissvoicesblog.wordpress.com/2012/08/17/boko-haram-is-no-african-al-qaeda/

III.

Messaging, Media, and the Masses

Supporters and Sympathizers

As detailed above, Boko Haram draws its domestic support largely from a population of northern Muslim Nigerians predisposed to tolerate Boko Haram or perhaps even support the group as a challenge to the federal state that has so badly failed to serve their interests. Even Nigeria's official figures demonstrate the severity of the problem. According to Nigeria's National Bureau of Statistics, "relative poverty was most apparent in Muslim dominated northern states… [almost] 70% of Nigerians in 2010 were living in 'absolute poverty'."[145] The trend leads experts to believe that the inequality in Nigeria is promoting widespread support of Boko Haram as the group has actively capitalized on these grievances in a conscious attempt to market themselves, using a number of tactics to attract support.[146]

Additionally, it is possible that skewed on-the-ground reporting distorts Boko Haram's image in the eyes of local northern Nigerians. Boko Haram has gone to great lengths to target and intimidate Nigerian journalists whose coverage they find unsatisfactory.[147] On the other hand, they have also worked with journalists they feel can represent them in a manner they approve – as was the case of Ahmad Salkida, a local journalist.[148] Salkida was able to establish a relationship with Boko Haram operatives in Maiduguri and received information directly from them. According to him, the resulting accuracy of his reporting led authorities to suspect he was a member of Boko Haram – which he denies. In 2009, he was arrested with Boko Haram members in the police crackdown that killed Mohammed Yusuf.[149] His anecdotes paint a grim picture, and at one point in April 2012 he publicly confirmed the existence of al Qaeda cells *within* Nigeria. Given Salkida's eyewitness accounts of Boko Haram, it is clear they are not shy about using media reporting to channel their message. In his own words, Salkida reiterates the problem with Boko Haram's widespread public support:

Another potential for disaster that may befall Nigeria is the massive recruitment into the nation's security agencies to contain the rising challenge of terrorism in the country. But nobody is paying attention to the very little background checks of the candidates that are now forming a battalion in the nation's defence force.[150]

---

[145] "Nigeria's Growing Poverty," Konye Obaji Ori, *The Africa Report,* February 14, 2012. Available at: http://www.theafricareport.com/index.php/2012021450181576/west-africa/nigeria-s-growing-poverty-50181576.html.

[146] Ibid.

[147] "Reporting Terrorism in Africa: A Personal Experience with Boko Haram by Ahmad Salkida," Ahmad Salkida, *SaharaReporters.com,* April 19, 2012. Available at: http://saharareporters.com/article/reporting-terrorism-africaa-personal-experience-boko-haram-ahmad-salkida.

[148] Ibid.

[149] "Changing face of Nigeria's Boko Haram," Xan Rice, *Financial Times,* May 22, 2012. Available at: http://www ft.com/intl/cms/s/0/9d2ab750-9ac1-11e1-9c98-00144feabdc0.html#axzz248aAa7vB.

[150] Salkida, *supra* note 147.

In August 2012, the names of over sixty SSS personnel were posted online, along with addresses and financial information.[151] It is widely speculated this leak was posted by Boko Haram, and might be a demonstration of the extent to which they or their sympathizers have infiltrated the security services. With this in mind, it becomes clear that supporters and sympathizers of Boko Haram may extend beyond the average northern Nigerian, into the upper-reaches of Nigerian society. Late last year, Senator Mohammed Ali Ndume from Borno State, who had previously been appointed by President Jonathan to a committee to consider opening talks with Boko Haram, was arrested by Nigerian police and accused of failing to report attacks the group was planning to the authorities.[152, 153] Still, it is not necessarily surprising that northern Nigerian political leaders would cooperate with Boko Haram. Given the multiple instances of Boko Haram targeting Muslim leaders for death, and the ruthlessness with which they dispatch with internal dissent, northern Nigerian Muslim leaders are no doubt under threat from Boko Haram. For example, the former governor of Kano State, Ibrahim Shekarau, allegedly agreed in late 2004 to make monthly payments of 5 million naira (approximately $31,500), which was later increased to 10 million naira (approximately $63,000) in 2009, to Boko Haram in order to have his state left alone.[154, 155] Similarly, Governor Isa Yuguda of Bauchi State had also allegedly agreed to Boko Haram's monthly bribe payments of 10 million naira (approximately $63,000) in 2008.[156]

Even more evidence of Boko Haram receiving payments from northern politicians appeared following the 2011 arrest of a spokesman for the group named Ali Sanda Umar Konduga.[157] Following SSS interrogation, Konduga disclosed the names of numerous politicians who he claimed had financially supported the group, including former Nigerian Ambassador to Sao Tome and Principe Saidu Pindar. On November 21, 2011, Senator Ndume was arrested by the SSS for also supporting Boko Haram.[158] Reports suggest some northern politicians have used Boko Haram as, in essence, political assassins, to eliminate their competition. Of course, this makes it difficult to identify reliable regional partners to stand against Boko Haram, which is a major roadblock to countering the threat they pose, as explained below.

---

[151] "AP Exclusive: Nigeria Secret Police Details Leaked," Josh Gambrell and Bashir Adigun, *Associated Press,* August 30, 2012. Available at: http://bigstory.ap.org/article/ap-exclusive-nigeria-secret-police-details-leaked.

[152] "Nigeria Moving to Confront Boko Haram Terrorism," *Voice of America,* November 13, 2011. Available at: http://www.voanews.com/content/nigeria-moving-to-confront-boko-haram-terrorism-134042033/148350 html.

[153] "Nigeria: Ndume Charged With Terror Acts," Atika Balal, *The Daily Trust,* December 13, 2011. Available at: http://allafrica.com/stories/201112130392 html.

[154] "Boko Haram: Shekarau Denies Monthly Donation," *THISDAY Live,* January 29, 2012. Available at: http://www.thisdaylive.com/articles/boko-haram-shekarau-denies-monthly-donation/108119/

[155] "We're on Northern govs' payroll – Boko Haram," *Vanguard,* January 27, 2012. Available at: http://www.vanguardngr.com/2012/01/we-re-on-northern-govspayroll-boko-haram/.

[156] Ibid.

[157] "Boko Haram: Detained Senator Admits Knowing BH Spokesperson," *Sahara Reporters*, November 22, 2011. Available at: http://mobile.saharareporters.com/news-page/boko-haram-detained-senator-admits-knowing-bh-spokesperson?page=4.

[158] "Nigeria: Ndume Moves to Abort Trial," *THISDAY Live,* March 22, 2012. Available at: http://allafrica.com/stories/201203220630 html.

IV.

Countering the Threat – Options for the US, Nigeria, and the International Community

Progress Made and Challenges Ahead

Any attempts to neutralize Boko Haram will undoubtedly require the implementation of a comprehensive plan for addressing not only the group's operational capability and the degraded security environment, but also tackling some of the grievous *long-term* crises of economy, governance, and societal tensions described above.[159]

Arguably, the most immediate of these concerns is the need to improve the professionalization and competence of Nigerian police and armed forces while degrading the operational capability of Boko Haram. Speaking at the Center for Strategic and International Studies on April 9, 2012, former Assistant Secretary of State Carson noted that, "more sophisticated and targeted security efforts are necessary to contain Boko Haram's acts of violence and to capture and prosecute its leaders."[160] In an effort to stay ahead of Boko Haram's improving tactics, so too must the Nigerian government further improve their own law enforcement and security operations. It therefore remains in the best interest of the United States to lend support to the Nigerian government in training and professionalizing Nigerian National Police, and military, as well as assisting in combatting corruption and improving quality of life and governance in Nigeria.

On its own, the Jonathan administration has taken some potentially promising steps in its efforts to fight Boko Haram. Acknowledging these advances is entirely necessary to comprehensively identify remaining gaps in Nigeria's approach. First and foremost, the appointment of Col. Sambo Dasuki (Ret.), a northern Nigerian Muslim, to the position of National Security Advisor on June 23, 2012, demonstrates that President Jonathan is willing to give northerners and Muslims a visible role in Nigeria's struggle with Boko Haram.[161] Dasuki has taken the lead in organizing the Nigerian federal government's fight against Boko Haram, and his background as a Muslim from the north may give him obvious and potent symbolic significance. To capitalize on that development, NSA Dasuki traveled throughout northern Nigeria after his appointment, meeting with local leaders and reminding northern Nigerians he was one of them.[162] President Jonathan's administration remains southern-dominated, but an increased role for northern players is a welcome step in establishing mutual interest in fighting Boko Haram.

On a more tactical level, the periodic capture of Boko Haram members and leaders not only removes operators from their ranks, but frequently provides a source of information to Nigerian services on the group's internal dynamics and operations. A prime example of such progress is the arrest of Boko Haram spokesman, "Abu Qaqa."[163]

---

[159] Carson, *supra* note 122.

[160] Ibid.

[161] "Sambo Dasuki - New Face of Nigerian Security," Heather Murdock, *Voice of America*, July 12, 2012. Available at: http://www.voanews.com/content/sambo-dasuki-new-face-nigerian-security/1403681.html.

[162] Ibid.

[163] "Nigeria: Abu Qaqa Confesses in Custody," Ike Abonyi, *THISDAY*, February 4, 2012. Available at: http://allafrica.com/stories/201202061862.html.

It is possible that the capture of leaders such as Suleiman Mohammed in May 2012, and other operatives can offer a window into the group's situation at that time.[164] Earlier this year, seven Boko Haram members were arrested after it was discovered that they were in possession of explosives manuals, propaganda leaflets, and information on al Qaeda in the Islamic Maghreb (AQIM) members they were planning on meeting.[165] Considering the fact that the members were en route to Mali via Niger, it would appear that these arrests could enhance counterterrorism cooperation on the parts of the Nigerien and Nigerian governments.

Nevertheless, concerns regarding the capability of the Jonathan Administration to effectively deal with Boko Haram remain prominent. One skeptic, Freedom C. Onuoha of the African Center for Strategic Research and Studies, states that the Jonathan Administration "will need international assistance, especially in the areas of intelligence sharing, counterinsurgency operations, detection of improvised explosive devices, forensic analysis, intelligence gathering and analysis, and the mounting of a de-radicalization program."[166] According to this perspective, without foreign assistance from countries such as the U.S. and the U.K., the Nigerian government will almost certainly face a prolonged battle in neutralizing Boko Haram.

Courses of Action for the Jonathan Administration

The scale of reforms necessary to limit social unrest across Nigeria is massive. These reforms must be undertaken in coordination with a simultaneous effort to eradicate Boko Haram. President Jonathan seems to view himself as the newest participant of the Nigerian "zoning" arrangement – wherein the presidency, and therefore all of the political patronage that goes with it – changes hands between the country's geographic regions at the end of each term. Yet Northern Muslims view his current term as a failure to abide by the same arrangement, given that his now-deceased predecessor had only served one term. With both halves of the country claiming a right to the presidency this term, it does not appear this arrangement can be maintained. The results of legitimate elections must be respected, however, President Jonathan should also take care to enfranchise the entire political establishment, not simply southern allies. The selection of Col. Dasuki as NSA is the first step, but more can and should be done to demonstrate trust in northern leaders.

Perhaps under those circumstances, ongoing and hugely important anti-corruption efforts can succeed to a greater degree. The consensus among most observers is that the high level of corruption in Nigeria weakens the government's legitimacy, and must be tackled to restore public confidence in Nigeria's government.

---

[164] "Nigeria soldiers arrest Boko Haram commander," Ibrahim Garba, *The Christian Science Monitor*, May 11, 2012. Available at: http://www.csmonitor.com/World/Africa/2012/0511/Nigeria-soldiers-arrest-Boko-Haram-commander.

[165] "Arms from Libya could reach Boko Haram, al Qaeda: UN," Louis Charbonneau, *Reuters,* January 27, 2012. Available at: http://af.reuters.com/article/topNews/idAFJOE80Q01420120127?sp=true.

[166] Bartolotta, *supra* note 120.

As the second-largest African recipient of bilateral U.S. development aid and the fifth largest recipient worldwide (not including assistance provided through Overseas Contingency Operations), Nigeria probably requires U.S. assistance to solve these and other problems. [167] The State Department's FY2014 security assistance request specifically includes roughly $1.7 million split between Foreign Military Financing (FMF) and military education and training. [168] In the House Committee on Homeland Security Subcommittee on Counterterrorism and Intelligence's previous report, it was noted that the U.S. Department of Defense (DOD) was working with the Nigerian military to enhance the training and professionalization of its forces. Examples of this cooperation include the U.S. Navy's African Partnership Station as part of a larger effort to enhance security in the Gulf of Guinea; the National Guard State Partnership Program (in which Nigeria participates); and the previous provision of counterterrorism funding ($2.2 million for the development of a counterterrorism infantry unit, and another $6.2 million designated to the tactical communications and interoperability within its counterterrorism unit). [169] The State Department, which has also engaged Nigeria through its African Coastal and Border Security (ACBS) program, has focused its assistance on peacekeeping support, training, border and maritime security, and increasing military professionalization. [170] Additionally, Nigeria is among the first targeted recipients for the new joint DOD and State Department-funded Global Security Contingency Fund (GSCF).

This assistance is vital – yet Nigeria's JTF continues to behave unprofessionally, and has been accused of human rights abuses by Human Rights Watch, among other entities, Including the State Department's most recent annual human rights report. [171] Greater pressure must be applied to Nigerian security forces to abandon counterproductive and brutal tactics that alienate Nigeria's northerners.

Beyond standard counterterrorism training, there are other areas in which Nigerian security services, including the police, could benefit from U.S. assistance. Boko Haram has murdered many Nigerian Muslim leaders who have stood up for peace. This eliminates allies in fighting Boko Haram and discourages other Nigerians from working with the Nigerian government. U.S. training could be provided to enhance the dignitary protection capabilities of the Nigerian security services in preserving these Muslim leaders from slaughter by Boko Haram – both preserving anti-Boko Haram voices and providing a symbol of the Jonathan administration's willingness to work with Nigeria's Muslim population.

It remains unlikely that the U.S. will be able to provide significant on-the-ground assistance to the JTF. Such assistance could also provide Boko Haram with a longer

---

[167] "The FY2014 State and Foreign Operations Budget Request," Susan B. Epstein, Marion Leonardo Lawson, Alex Tiersky, *Congressional Research Service,* May 2, 2013. Available at: http://www fas.org/sgp/crs/row/R43043.pdf.

[168] "Executive Budget Summary: Function 150 & Other International Programs," *U.S. Department of State,* April 10, 2013. Available at: http://www.state.gov/documents/organization/207305.pdf.

[169] Ploch, *supra* note 22, at 25.

[170] Ibid.

[171] "Spiraling Violence: Boko Haram Attacks and Security Force Abuses in Nigeria," *Human Rights Watch,* October 2012. Available at: http://www.hrw.org/sites/default/files/reports/nigeria1012webwcover.pdf.

target list and a messaging opportunity. However, it also continues to be critical that the U.S. work more closely with Nigerian security forces to develop greater domestic intelligence collection and sharing with the U.S. Intelligence Community. According to a report released by the Joint Special Operations University, the Nigerian government has employed an "organizational decapitation approach," in going after Boko Haram.[172] This approach bears some resemblance to the broader U.S. strategy to defeat al Qaeda. In its previous report, the Subcommittee on Counterterrorism and Intelligence suggested that such a model (using counterterrorism efforts in Yemen as an example) could be applied to Boko Haram. Yet the public executions and seemingly indiscriminate abuse of their authority by Nigerian police and Nigerian security forces have rendered this strategy ineffective.

Media reports have noted calls for expanding the U.S. drone program in areas like West Africa, specifically to combat AQIM.[173] If such an expansion were to take place, the use of surveillance drones to assist our allies in degrading AQIM in Mali might have an impact on their ally, Boko Haram. Already, reports that the French effort to fight the insurgency in Mali utilized American assistance by way of surveillance drones certainly demonstrate a future for U.S. aerial vehicles in the Sahel.[174] This is one potential avenue for the U.S. to assist Nigeria to combat Boko Haram and other al Qaeda affiliates in the region.

Increased Intelligence Collection and the Importance of AFRICOM

In his prepared answers provided to SASC before February 2013 confirmation hearing, General Rodriguez acknowledged, "AFRICOM receives only about 7% of its total intelligence, surveillance, and reconnaissance requirements."[175] If this figure is accurate, some have noted that it would require an almost 15-fold increase in collection to meet AFRICOM's requirements fully.[176] Given current budgetary constraints, it is difficult to imaging that these needs will be fully met in the short-term. At the same time, however, given the diversifying threat throughout Africa, it is also hard to believe that many have suggested dissolving AFRICOM entirely.[177]

Splitting AFRICOM apart after only five years in existence would represent a major step back in our national security efforts in the region. The effectiveness and survival of programs under AFRICOM's leadership would be caste into doubt, leaving our regional partners with mixed signals about our commitment to helping them

---

[172] "Confronting the Terrorism of Boko Haram in Nigeria," James J.F. Forest, Ph.D., *The Joint Special Operations University*, May 05, 2012, pg. 91. Available at: http://www.jamesforest.com/wp-content/uploads/2012/06/Boko_Haram_JSOU-Report-2012.pdf.

[173] "White House urged to boost CIA drone fleet," *United Press International,* October 19, 2012. Available at: http://www.upi.com/Top_News/US/2012/10/26/White-House-urged-to-boost-CIA-drone-fleet/UPI-32991350628200/#ixzz2BkmfKvxT.

[174] "AP Exclusive: France to send drones to Mali region," *Associated Press,* October 22, 2012. Available at: http://news.yahoo.com/ap-exclusive-france-send-drones-mali-region-200931532.html.

[175] General Rodriguez, *supra* note 92.

[176] "Pirate Threat Grows Worse off West Africa," *Defensenews,* May 3, 2013. Available at: http://www.defensenews.com/article/20130503/DEFREG04/304290023/Pirate-Threat-Grows-Worse-off-West-Africa.

[177] "DoD Weighs Major COCOM Realignment," *DefenseNews,* August 11, 2013. Available at: http://www.defensenews.com/apps/pbcs.dll/article?AID=2013308110001.

overcome their security challenges. Particularly in the case of Boko Haram, where success is likely to be predicated on partnering with the Nigerian government to ensure their security services can address the threat competently, an end to AFRICOM would limit our ability to help our allies achieve victory.

Advances in Diplomatic Engagement

The United States has an interest in helping Nigeria address their long-term problems. Toward that end, the U.S. Agency for International Development (USAID) has continued to operate their programs in the northern states of Bauchi and Sokoto, which began before Boko Haram's reemergence.[178] Nigeria also serves as a minor partner in the Trans-Sahara Counterterrorism Partnership (TSCTP), a State Department initiative aimed at helping a number of African countries in the Trans-Sahara and Sahel regions combat terrorist organizations.[179]

Over the last several years, many have called for the United States to build up our diplomatic presence in the north. For his part, Ambassador McCulley has reiterated the desire to expand American public outreach to the north by opening a consulate in Kano.[180] Yet, the Ambassador also noted that the security environment and budgetary constraints mean it will be some time before this is a viable option. Nonetheless, this could be a way to improve the image of the United States and our allies in the long-term in the eyes of northern Nigerians, and should be seriously considered.

The United States should continue to advocate for the recognition of the grievances of the northern Nigerian population. Perhaps most importantly in the short-term, the United States should take allegations of human rights abuses by Nigerian security forces very seriously. While Nigeria's military and police have an obligation to end Boko Haram, they have a responsibility to treat innocent citizens humanely. As former Assistant Secretary Carson publicly declared, "Security efforts aimed that [sic] containing Boko Haram's violence must avoid excessive violence and human right abuses and make better use of police and intelligent services to identify, to arrest and to prosecute those responsible for Boko Haram's violent acts."[181] Similar emphasis on responsible tactics should be employed by all U.S. entities working with Nigeria.

Since 2010, the U.S.-Nigeria Binational Commission has served as an avenue for dialogue between Washington and Abuja on multiple issues of importance.[182] The

---

[178] "Testimony of Assistant Administrator for Africa, Earl Gast, Before the House Subcommittee on African Affairs," Earl Gast, U.S.Agency for International Development, July 10, 2012. Available at: http://www.usaid.gov/news-information/congressional-testimony/testimony-assistant-administrator-africa-earl-gast-house.

[179] "The Trans-Sahara Counterterrorism Partnership," *U.S. Africa Command website,* http://www.africom.mil/tsctp.asp. TSCTP partners include Algeria, Morocco, Tunisia, Chad, Mauritania, Niger, Nigeria, and Senegal.

[180] "US Wants to Open Consulate to Reach Northern Nigerians," Lekan Oyekanmi, *Voice of America*, April 3, 2012. Available at: http://www.voanews.com/content/us-wants-to-open-consulate-to-reach-northern-nigerians-146141775/180821 html.

[181] "House Foreign Affairs Subcommittee on Africa, Global Health and Human Rights Holds Hearing on the U.S. Policy Toward Nigeria," Johnnie Carson, Assistant Secretary of African Affairs, *CQ Congressional Transcripts*, July 10, 2012. Available at: http://www.cq.com/doc/congressionaltranscripts-4120793?wr=Q1U4djBRbm5MbW0wYkYta2NQQ2dtZw.

[182] Ibid., 23.

Commission held a summit at the United States Institute of Peace (USIP) in June 2012, and released a joint communiqué outlining areas of continued cooperation.[183] The agreements included in the joint communiqué address multiple areas of concern, and the U.S. committed itself to "help strengthen the capacity of the Nigerian Police Force to effectively control and investigate serious crimes while respecting human rights..."[184] The Binational Commission also promised to establish a "sub-working group" to assist the Nigerian government's effort to establish a fusion center for intelligence collection, analysis and dissemination. According to the *Voice of America*, during an August 2012 trip to Abuja, Secretary of State Clinton offered a proposal to help Nigeria establish this center, based on similar fusion centers within the US.[185] In November 2012, the Nigerian government formally requested assistance to do so, and in December 2012 a group of Embassy officials and the staff of the Office of the National Security Adviser met to determine how the U.S. can support Nigeria's efforts to develop its intelligence fusion capability.[186] It is unclear where the creation of the center stands at present, or exactly how the Department of State will work with the Nigerian government to develop this entity, but this effort is a positive, proactive step to assisting the Nigerians in defeating Boko Haram.

Foreign Terrorist Organization (FTO) Designation

The Secretary of State has not yet designated Boko Haram a Foreign Terrorist Organization (FTO). It has become clear that Boko Haram merits such a designation, and the continued failure to acknowledge this fact is the most obvious flaw in the U.S. effort to combat Boko Haram and prevent their expansion. While the State Department may have designated three leaders within Boko Haram as SDGTs, the legal ramifications of this decision are relatively limited. As a result of the SDGT designations, any property of the three Boko Haram leaders was barred from U.S. jurisdiction, and U.S. persons were prohibited "from engaging in transactions with or for the benefit of these individuals."[187] In effect, support provided to Boko Haram that is not directly tied to these three terrorists remains legal. It is also worthy of note that if these individuals are killed or captured and subsequently replaced by other Boko Haram members, there will be no legal prohibitions against aiding Boko Haram within U.S. territory. While the SDGT designations of Shekau, Kambar, and al-Barnawi are positive steps, they are not productive enough, and ultimately do little to sanction the group as a whole.

In the House Committee on Homeland Security's Subcommittee on Counterterrorism and Intelligence's previous report, it was noted that the "Office of the

---

[183] "U.S., Nigeria Sign Communiqué on Bilateral Cooperation at USIP," *The United States Institute of Peace*, June 6, 2012. Available at: http://www.usip.org/publications/us-nigeria-sign-communique-bilateral-cooperation-usip.

[184] "Terrorist Designations of Boko Haram Commander Abubakar Shekau, Khalid al-Barnawi and Abubakar Adam Kambar," Office of the Spokesperson, *U.S. Department of State,* June 21, 2012. Available at: http://www.state.gov/r/pa/prs/ps/2012/06/193574 htm.

[185] "Clinton Offers Aid to Nigerian Security Forces Against Boko Haram," Anne Look, *Voice of America,* August 9, 2012. Available at: http://www.voanews.com/content/clinton-nigeria-boko-haram/1483662.html.

[186] "Country Reports on Terrorism 2012," Office of the Coordinator for Counterterrorism, May 30, 2013. Available at: http://www.state.gov/j/ct/rls/crt/2012/

[187] U.S. Department of State, *supra* note 184.

Coordinator for Counterterrorism in the State Department (S/CT) continually monitors the activities of terrorist groups active around the world to identify potential targets for designation. When reviewing targets of specific groups, S/CT looks not only at the actual terrorist attacks that a group has carried out, but also at whether the group has engaged in planning and preparations for possible future acts of terrorism or retains the capability and intent to carry out such acts."[188]

The legal criteria for FTO designation includes the following:

1. It must be a foreign organization.
2. The organization must engage in terrorist activity, as defined in section 212 (a)(3)(B) of the INA (8 U.S.C. § 1182(a)(3)(B)),* or terrorism, as defined in section 140(d)(2) of the Foreign Relations Authorization Act, Fiscal Years 1988 and 1989 (22 U.S.C. § 2656f(d)(2)),** or retain the capability and intent to engage in terrorist activity or terrorism.
3. The organization's terrorist activity or terrorism must threaten the security of U.S. nationals or the national security (national defense, foreign relations, or the economic interests) of the United States.

Boko Haram clearly meets these criteria. If Boko Haram were to be designated an FTO, it would support U.S. Intelligence Community efforts to curb the group's financing, stigmatize and isolate it internationally, heighten public awareness and knowledge, and signal to other governments the U.S. takes the threat from Boko Haram seriously.[189] If Boko Haram is not designated an FTO, its potential threat to the U.S. and its capability to attack the homeland would likely increase. It is therefore an urgent next step to take in fighting this growing al Qaeda affiliate in Nigeria.

In January 2012, Assistant Attorney General Lisa Monaco sent a letter to Ambassador Daniel Benjamin, head of the State Department's Bureau of Counterterrorism urging that Boko Haram be designated an FTO. [190] Such a letter is an obvious indicator of the need to add Boko Haram to the FTO list. Failure to do so is a failure to heed the lessons of Al Qaeda in the Arabian Peninsula (AQAP) and the Tehrik-i-Taliban Pakistan (TTP). Both of these networks were not made FTOs until after they attempted attacks against the U.S. Homeland. Given Boko Haram's trajectory, it is reasonable to fear they could attempt something similar. If this were the case, an FTO designation could help to mitigate the threat. Though not a cure-all for the danger Boko Haram poses to the United States and U.S. interests, an FTO designation encourages nations around the world to impose their own sanctions on Boko Haram. The United States can and should be a leader in the effort to cut off Boko Haram's resources and prevent them from expanding their support.

---

[188] Complete information regarding legal criteria for FTO designation can be found at the website of the U.S. Department of State, Office of Coordinator for Counterterrorism. Available at: http://www.state.gov/s/ct/rls/other/des/123085.htm.

[189] U.S. Department of State, *supra* note 184.

[190] "US debates 'terrorist' sanctions for Nigerian militants," Mark Hosenball and John Shiffman, *Reuters,* May 25, 2012. Available at: http://articles.chicagotribune.com/2012-05-25/business/sns-rt-usa-securitybokoharaml1e8gp87e-20120525_1_terrorist-designation-foreign-terrorist-group-nigerian-security-forces.

The State Department and Obama Administration have already identified Boko Haram as a terrorist organization, yet withhold formal designation. Most recently, in May 2013, Secretary of State John Kerry stated that, "Boko Haram is a terrorist organization and they have killed wantonly and upset the normal governance of Nigeria in fundamental ways that are unacceptable."[191] Just a few days earlier, the State Department released a press statement "condemn[ing] Boko Haram's campaign of terror in the strongest terms," following increased fighting in the region.[192] The 2013 International Narcotics Control Strategy Report, released by the State Department on July 1, 2013, also calls out Boko Haram as part of a growing threat in Niger, noting "more recent factors affecting security are the return of pro-Qaddafi mercenaries, the takeover of western neighbor Mali by al Qaida and affiliates, and the terrorist organization Boko Haram based in southern neighbor Nigeria."[193]

Boko Haram is becoming an increasing priority for the Obama Administration. Secretary Kerry met with the Nigerian Foreign Minister in April 2013, and according to Acting Deputy Spokesperson Patrick Ventrell, "they did discuss Boko Haram in some detail.... Boko Haram was very much on the agenda."[194] In April 2012, John Brennan, then-Assistant to the President for Homeland Security and Counterterrorism, said that "in Nigeria, we are monitoring closely the emergence of Boko Haram, a group that appears to be aligning itself with al-Qa'ida's violent agenda and is increasingly looking to attack Western interests in Nigeria in addition to Nigerian government targets."[195] As the number of attacks perpetrated by Boko Haram has increased in 2013, so has the attention paid to the group by the U.S. The State Department's 2012 Country Reports on Terrorism, released in May 2013, states that "the presence of the violent extremist group Boko Haram (BH) in northern Nigeria, just across Niger's southern border, posed a threat" and noted that "of particular concern to the United States is the emergence of the BH faction known as "Ansaru," which has close ties to AQIM and has prioritized targeting Westerners – including Americans – in Nigeria."[196] The report acknowledges that this threat is growing, noting that "elements of BH increased the number and sophistication of attacks...with a notable increase in the lethality, capability, and coordination of attacks."[197]

[191] "Remarks with Ethiopian Foreign Minister Tedros Adhanom After Their Meeting," John Kerry, May 25, 2013. Available at: http://www.state.gov/secretary/remarks/2013/05/209963 htm.

[192] "State of Emergency and Fighting in Northern Nigeria," John Kerry, May 17, 2013. Available at: http://www.state.gov/secretary/remarks/2013/05/209576.htm.

[193] "2013 International Narcotics Control Strategy Report (INCSR)—Volume II: Money Laundering and Financial Crimes Country Database—Montenegro through Suriname," *Bureau of International Narcotics and Law Enforcement Affairs,* July 1, 2013. Available at: http://www.state.gov/j/inl/rls/nrcrpt/2013/database/211183 htm.

[194] "Daily Press Briefing," Patrick Ventrell, April 25, 2013. Available at: http://www.state.gov/r/pa/prs/dpb/2013/04/208007.htm#NIGERIA

[195] "The Ethics and Efficacy of the President's Counterterrorism Strategy," John O. Brennan, April 30, 2012. Available at: http://www.state.gov/documents/organization/211953.pdf

[196] "Country Reports on Terrorism 2012," Office of the Coordinator for Counterterrorism, May 30, 2013. Available at: http://www.state.gov/j/ct/rls/crt/2012/

[197] Ibid.

V.

CONCLUSION

For years, Boko Haram has assaulted the people of Nigeria, embraced al Qaeda's brand of international terror, and threatened the United States. While there is no evidence that al Qaeda's core in Afghanistan and Pakistan commands Boko Haram's operations, it is clear from the words of multiple U.S. officials, media reports, and their own public statements, that Boko Haram is supportive of, and supported by, al Qaeda networks such as AQIM. Above all, it is the unity of ideology and mutual hatred for the West between these two groups that exposes the danger Boko Haram poses to the U.S. Homeland.

While Boko Haram began as, and maintains elements of, a basic Islamist movement, it has evolved into a hardened and sophisticated terror network. The challenge for Nigeria and its partners is to arrest and incarcerate or eliminate Boko Haram operatives, while at the same time shrinking their broad public sympathy among northern Nigerian Muslims. This is a complex obstacle, and requires multiple simultaneous efforts to enhance the capability of Nigeria's police and military, restore the trust in Nigeria's government among large segments of its population, and provide viable solutions to the long-term problems faced by many Nigerians in the north.

The world is coming to know more about Boko Haram; their intentions, what they're capable of, and who is supporting them. The U.S. Intelligence Community is working to erase the gaps in our understanding of Boko Haram, but it is already evident they are a serious threat to U.S. interests and potentially to the U.S. Homeland. Acknowledging this threat publicly by designating Boko Haram an FTO will establish a legal mechanism for prosecuting any supporters within U.S. jurisdictions. This is an increasingly important tool given their attempts to market themselves to a wider international audience.

Boko Haram shows no signs of ending its campaign against the government of Nigeria and the Western world. Two years after their August 2011 bombing of a U.N. facility in Abuja, Nigeria, Boko Haram remains a threat to the international community, and continues to be a developing threat to the U.S. Homeland.

www.ingramcontent.com/pod-product-compliance
Lightning Source LLC
Chambersburg PA
CBHW080636290526
45790CB00007B/3082